Web Applications with Elm

Functional Programming for the Web

Wolfgang Loder

Apress®

Web Applications with Elm: Functional Programming for the Web

Wolfgang Loder
Vienna, Austria

ISBN-13 (pbk): 978-1-4842-2609-4   ISBN-13 (electronic): 978-1-4842-2610-0
https://doi.org/10.1007/978-1-4842-2610-0

Library of Congress Control Number: 2018954229

Managing Director, Apress Media LLC: Welmoed Spahr
Acquisitions Editor: Steve Anglin
Development Editor: Matthew Moodie
Coordinating Editor: Mark Powers

Cover designed by eStudioCalamar

Cover image designed by Freepik (www.freepik.com)

Distributed to the book trade worldwide by Springer Science+Business Media New York, 233 Spring Street, 6th Floor, New York, NY 10013. Phone 1-800-SPRINGER, fax (201) 348-4505, email orders-ny@springer-sbm.com, or visit www.springeronline.com. Apress Media, LLC is a California LLC and the sole member (owner) is Springer Science + Business Media Finance Inc (SSBM Finance Inc). SSBM Finance Inc is a **Delaware** corporation.

For information on translations, please email editorial@apress.com; for reprint, paperback, or audio rights, please email bookpermissions@springernature.com.

Apress titles may be purchased in bulk for academic, corporate, or promotional use. eBook versions and licenses are also available for most titles. For more information, reference our Print and eBook Bulk Sales web page at http://www.apress.com/bulk-sales.

Any source code or other supplementary material referenced by the author in this book is available to readers on GitHub via the book's product page, located at www.apress.com/9781484226094. For more detailed information, please visit http://www.apress.com/source-code.

Printed on acid-free paper

Table of Contents

About the Author

 **Wolfgang Loder** has been programming software since the 1980s. He successfully rejected all calls to fill management roles and remained hands-on until now. His journey went from assembler and C to C++ and Java to C# and F# and JavaScript, from Waterfall to Agile, from Imperative to Declarative, and other paradigm changes too numerous to list and remember. For most of his career Wolfgang was a contracting enterprise developer, a field where the introduction of "new" languages, frameworks, and concepts is very slow. Once he decided to develop his own products he was free of such constraints and ventured into all sorts of paradigms, be it NoSQL or functional, evaluating all the latest ideas, crazy or not. In other words, he has fun developing software. Wolfgang was born in Vienna and lives in Austria.

About the Technical Reviewer

Aleks Drozdov is an architect, team lead, and software engineer with more than 20 years of experience in analysis, design, and implementation of complex information systems using Lean Architecture and Agile methodologies. He has extensive practical knowledge in service-oriented technologies; distributed and parallel systems; relational, non-relational, and graph databases; data search, and analytics. Aleks likes to learn new technologies and isn't afraid of starting a new project in a new field. He is spending his time designing and implementing digital preservation systems and exploring the field of machine learning and artificial intelligence. In his free time, he likes to read history books, take long walks, play guitar, and spend time with his grandkids.

CHAPTER 1

Introduction

In 2012, the first versions of a new functional language were published. It was based on Haskell and was called *Elm*; it was mentioned here and there as one of the upcoming programming languages for the web.

A few years later, I came across the term *reactive programming*. At that time Facebook's React framework was becoming the latest hype, and similar frameworks were popping up in the user-interface development space. Reactive user interfaces are nothing new—they were researched before graphical interfaces were mainstream. I became interested in knowing more about how this decades-old paradigm was being applied to modern web-based user interfaces.

One topic and search result led to another, and soon the name *Evan Czaplicki*[1] came up. He had written a thesis about *functional reactive programming (FRP)* and created the Elm language to implement the ideas in the thesis. At that stage—about version 0.14—the Elm platform was very basic, but many developers could see the potential.

My research of the reactive paradigm coincided with a project I was doing at that time, a digital asset repository. The implementation of the project's back end was the base for the book *Erlang and Elixir for Imperative Programmers*.[2] That project also needed a web client, and I was thinking: What a good chance to use Elm for a real-life project!

I have used Elm in several projects now, most of them internal applications for companies that appreciate the quick turnaround from design to implementation and do not need extravagant user interfaces with the latest style frameworks. What they need, though, are applications that do what they are supposed to do without having runtime errors at the most inconvenient times. And Elm is delivering just that.

---

[1]https://twitter.com/czaplic
[2]http://www.apress.com/gp/book/9781484223932

© Wolfgang Loder 2018
W. Loder, *Web Applications with Elm*, https://doi.org/10.1007/978-1-4842-2610-0_1

1

Fast forwarding to 2018, Evan Czaplicki has changed the architecture of Elm to make it "easier to learn and use"[3] and also to further emphasize concurrency. This was a change in version 0.17. At the time of writing this book, version 0.18 is the latest implementation of Elm.

Elm is not complete, but it is used in production, and the community is getting bigger. Whether Elm can get into the mainstream is not yet clear, but it certainly can carve out a niche in the very competitive world of front-end development.

This chapter will give you a taste of Elm. It is not a presentation of the syntax or the tools, which we will get to in subsequent chapters. It rather describes where the language is coming from and demonstrates what can be done with it.

At the end of the chapter, you—the reader—will have a basic idea of Elm as a programming platform, and hopefully you will be excited to dive deeper into the details.

Theory

Even if the creator of Elm says that it is not about functional reactive programming anymore, but rather about concurrency, it is worth having a quick look at the history of the reactive idea that dates back to the 1980s.

Any software program deals with the following scenario:

- A computer program has to process a stream of data.

- Data travels in an asynchronous way.

- Events are defined by time and data.

- A computer program has to react to events.

In addition, the programming of user interfaces has to cover the following:

- Users define events, for example by moving a pointer on the screen with a mouse.

- Users need to have a visible reaction to their actions.

Programming patterns and operating systems handle the preceding points by forcing the stream of data into a synchronous data flow. For example, we can use queues to save data and then deal with it sequentially. The time dimension of an event is not lost, but response time to an event can be anything from *immediate* to *never*.

---

[3]http://elm-lang.org/blog/farewell-to-frp

Problems occur when events affect data that other event handlers can access at the same time. We call this data the state of the program. Programmers are familiar with the problems of concurrency in imperative languages, either from having to deal with it themselves or from listening to stories told by fellow developers. Programming with functional languages is declarative programming: we say what we need and let the language and its libraries do the work. It makes programming easier and also more joyful.

From the preceding description we see why concurrency is an important—perhaps the most important—part of Elm. Making the programming of concurrent processes easier for the developer by pushing the handling of it into the platform has the added effect of reducing possible runtime errors.

Over the years, Elm has undergone changes to make first reactive and then concurrent concepts easier to apply. The language and platform as a whole have certainly advanced well since the first release. There is still some pain when newer versions introduce breaking changes, not only in the language, but also in the architecture.

In particular, both interfacing with JavaScript and event handling changed over time and made it necessary to reimplement existing code or learn new ways of implementing certain features. This book uses version 0.18, and I can say that the language has matured well. There are still pitfalls when integrating Elm into a website or debugging Elm applications, which we will get to later in this book.

At the time of writing, version 0.19 is developed. It is not clear when this version will go live, but it is expected sometime in 2018. In any case, we can expect more breaking changes as the Elm platform evolves.

What Can We Use Elm For?

When you see Elm and other frameworks and platforms competing in the same space, you may ask yourself the following:

- Why use Elm?

- Why learn Elm and then create JavaScript?

- Why use pure functional programming?

- Is there any advantage to using Elm?

The answers to these and similar questions are dependent on your own circumstances and requirements. The following paragraphs—and in fact the whole book—are based on my opinion, formed after experiencing Elm. I am positive that Elm is useful, but I am not so biased that I don't see the problems with the language and platform as they are at the time of writing this book.

So, what is Elm good for? Short answer: It is good for any web application that has interactions with its users. This is a very wide definition that puts almost all web applications into Elm's domain. Note that I am talking of web *applications*—websites with static content are not in that bucket. Of course, it is possible to use the Elm platform for those as well, but other languages and frameworks may be more useful. In Chapter 6 we will see if we can use Elm beyond web applications.

The diagram in Figure 1-1, which certainly is not exhaustive, shows some of the application types developers are using Elm for.

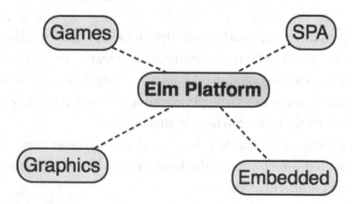

Figure 1-1. *What is Elm used for?*

Let's go through this list to see examples.

Games

Some of the first public examples of the use of Elm were, not surprisingly, browser-based games. For a long time, the Elm website had a *Mario* example prominently displayed on the examples page (see Figure 1-2). It disappeared after some time, probably for copyright reasons. Nevertheless, the idea that the combination of *reactive* and *concurrent* is good for a game is correct.

Figure 1-2. *Example Mario game*

The example is available *here*.[4] In a bit more than one hundred lines the program lets Mario walk, stand, and jump. It is basic but shows how the platform, with its language and libraries, helps to develop in a few lines an application that reacts to key input.

Beware   The example uses a deprecated feature called *signal*, which was superseded by a replacement feature called *subscription*. An implementation for version 0.18 is available *here*.[5]

Single-Page Applications (SPAs)

Single-page applications are perhaps the most common type of application that Elm is used for, although there are not too many known such applications in production—emphasis on "known," as there may be many applications we just don't know about that use Elm. My own applications are examples of "unknown" applications. They were implemented for specific customers and will likely never be available in the public space. Nevertheless, the architecture and the language of Elm assist in implementing applications that are less error prone than pure JavaScript implementations.

---

[4]http://elm-lang.org:1234/examples/mario
[5]https://github.com/avh4/elm-mario

The following screenshot (Figure 1-3) shows some forms of a "Pizza Order" app. It is from an example I was writing to help me evaluate a commercial JavaScript framework for styling and features.

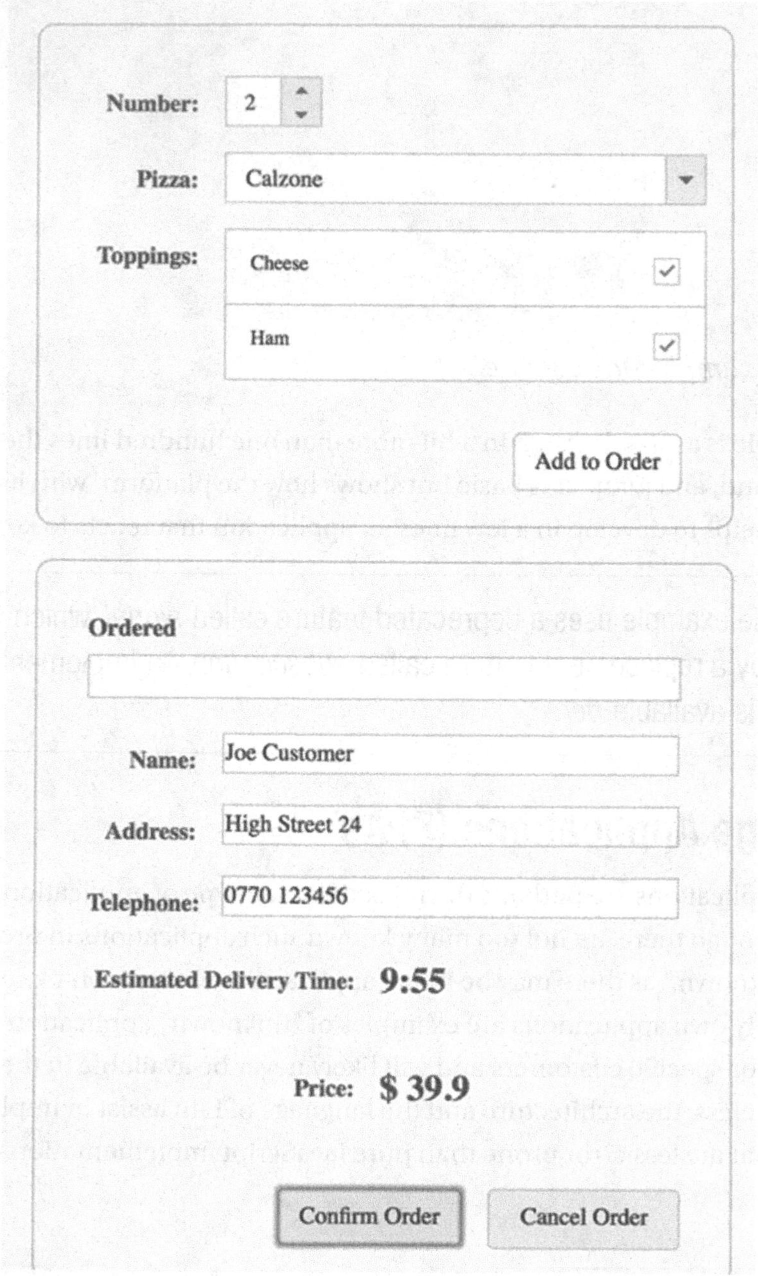

Figure 1-3. *Example forms*

This app makes heavy use of interfacing with JavaScript, which is not always necessary, but on the other side it is good to know it can be done.

What remains to be seen in the future is whether complicated applications can be done with Elm as well. My own experience shows that one runs against a wall from time to time or has to implement wrapper code in JavaScript. It is possible to move from SPAs to multi-page applications, though.

Graphics

The Elm platform provides powerful graphics libraries. One example of their capabilities is the *Mario* game. Another example is the Elm logo pictured in Figure 1-4.

Figure 1-4. *Example Elm logo*

This logo can be created using the SVG library with the code shown in Figure 1-5.

```
svg
  [ version "1.1", x "0", y "0", viewBox "0 0 323.141 322.95"
  ]
  [ polygon [ fill "#F0AD00", points "161.649,152.782 231.514,82.916 91.783,82.916" ] []
  , polygon [ fill "#7FD13B", points "8.867,0 79.241,70.375 232.213,70.375 161.838,0" ] []
  , rect
      [ fill "#7FD13B", x "192.99", y "107.392", width "107.676", height "108.167"
      , transform "matrix(0.7071 0.7071 -0.7071 0.7071 186.4727 -127.2386)"
      ]
      []
  , polygon [ fill "#60B5CC", points "323.298,143.724 323.298,0 179.573,0" ] []
  , polygon [ fill "#5A6378", points "152.781,161.649 0,8.868 0,314.432" ] []
  , polygon [ fill "#F0AD00", points "255.522,246.655 323.298,314.432 323.298,178.879" ] []
  , polygon [ fill "#60B5CC", points "161.649,170.517 8.869,323.298 314.43,323.298" ] []
  ]
```

Figure 1-5. *Example logo source code*

Compiling the Elm code and running it results in an SVG tag on the website (see Figure 1-6).

```
▼<svg version="1.1" x="0" y="0" viewBox="0 0 323.141 322.95">
    <polygon fill="#F0AD00" points="161.649,152.782 231.514,82.916 91.783,82.916"></polygon>
    <polygon fill="#7FD13B" points="8.867,0 79.241,70.375 232.213,70.375 161.838,0">
    </polygon>
    <rect fill="#7FD13B" x="192.99" y="107.392" width="107.676" height="108.167" transform=
    "matrix(0.7071 0.7071 -0.7071 0.7071 186.4727 -127.2386)"></rect>
    <polygon fill="#60B5CC" points="323.298,143.724 323.298,0 179.573,0"></polygon>
    <polygon fill="#5A6378" points="152.781,161.649 0,8.868 0,314.432"></polygon>
    <polygon fill="#F0AD00" points="255.522,246.655 323.298,314.432 323.298,178.879">
    </polygon>
    <polygon fill="#60B5CC" points="161.649,170.517 8.869,323.298 314.43,323.298"></polygon>
  </svg>
```

Figure 1-6. *Example logo SVG tag*

Embedded

Developers who want to introduce Elm may have difficulty getting approval from project managers. One way, as described on the Elm website, is to start by embedding small applications in existing websites.

Elm code can be compiled into JavaScript files, which can then be imported to an HTML page with the usual script tags. There is no issue with either embedding several compiled Elm files or using one file several times on a page. The only downside is that the Elm runtime will be embedded several times. It is not too big, but it would still be a waste of bandwidth.

Also, the embedded Elm applications have to be self-contained regarding state. Communication between them is only possible via JavaScript code and by interfacing with that code. Obviously, we may run into the concurrency problems that Elm tries to solve in the first place when we have to update the state of those embedded Elm applications.

What Can't We Do with Elm?

After all the positive examples in the preceding paragraphs, we should now discuss what we *can't* do with Elm. Again, I must provide the disclaimer that I am writing this book with version 0.18 in mind.

It is not completely true to say that there are requirements we can't implement with Elm, because we can do everything by interfacing with external JavaScript code on a website. Doing implementations this way is probably not in the spirit of Elm, and it also defies some of the strong points of Elm, like type safety and a compiler that makes sure certain functions are implemented before running the application.

By interfacing with external JavaScript we lose certain advantages. The result may be to reimplement features inside the Elm platform. Whether or not this makes sense is another question. Styling may be easier, but using a framework with enhanced component features forces the developer to write interface wrappers with their own models that can then be transferred into the Elm application.

Another problem with Elm is that it does not have any lifecycle hooks. Elm is not only a language, but also a runtime environment and more. A lifecycle hook into the Elm runtime would help to integrate it with third-party JavaScript libraries, but then we are discussing the question of interfacing again.

For example, when Elm renders the page and we want to run JavaScript on an element, we can't because the JavaScript code will not be called immediately during the render process. There are workarounds, as we will see later, but it could be easier.

Something else we can't do with Elm is embed it into console tools or use it on the server. This may be supported in the future, although it is not clear how far away this future is or if it is even something that should be added. Elm is not a general-purpose language, and having features like server rendering may break its clean architecture.

When describing all these problems we should not forget that Elm was created to do web applications—especially SPAs—and it is doing this well. As developers, we always want to push to the edges, of course.

Who Is This Book For?

This book is an introduction to programming Elm applications. It gives an overview of the language and shows how Elm can be used for web applications and beyond. I assume that most readers of this book are developers and know one or more programming languages but don't know much more about Elm than the examples on the Elm website.[6]

It helps if you know the basics of JavaScript, especially if you want to interface with existing JavaScript libraries. You don't need to know functional programming, however. After reading the book, you should have the knowledge needed to dive deeper into the Elm platform with more advanced learning material. Some developers even start learning Haskell and use learning Elm as an introduction to Haskell.

Required Software

The only requirement for this book is a computer that is running any of the big three operating systems (Linux, Mac OS, Windows). We will install everything necessary to develop Elm applications, and also discuss plug-ins for your favorite editor or IDE.

---

[6]http://elm-lang.org/examples

> **Note**   Elm is open source. If you want to compile your own version, you will have to set up a Haskell environment on your computer. The easiest way is to use a Docker container that has Haskell installed in it and take it from there. I did it on Mac OS without a container and did not have problems, as I followed *this information*[7] in Elm's repository.

All source code will be available for readers of this book to download.

Structure of This Book

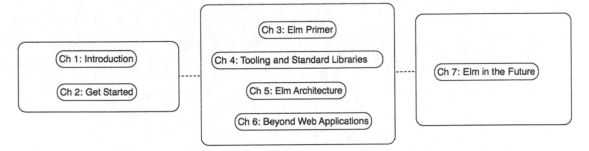

Figure 1-7. *Book Overview*

Chapters 2 to 4 will provide a primer of the language and the platform's tools and libraries. It won't be enough to be able to write big applications, but it is a start.

Chapter 2 will also set up our development environment. We will install Elm and prepare our favorite editor for Elm programming.

In Chapter 5 we will dive deeper into the building blocks of applications. After explaining the Elm architecture, we will discuss certain features non-trivial web applications need, like styling, forms, security, or access to third-party APIs. Since Elm has its own runtime it needs to interface with regular JavaScript code, which we will look into in this part of the book as well.

Chapter 6 will try to look beyond web applications and discuss how and if the Elm platform can be used for desktop applications or on the back end.

In Chapter 7 we will have a look at what the future may bring for Elm.

---

[7]https://github.com/elm-lang/elm-platform

CHAPTER 2

Getting Started

In Chapter 1 we saw examples of Elm applications and also had a glimpse into what can be achieved with the Elm platform. Those applications either used Elm on its own or integrated Elm with JavaScript libraries and frameworks.

Our goal is to develop applications like the ones featured in this book. Before we can enjoy the fun of doing this, we first have to invest some time in learning the basics of the Elm platform. This book gives a comprehensive introduction to the Elm platform on which you can base the implementation of your first Elm applications.

In this chapter, we will look at the following topics:

- Installing the Elm platform

- Deciding on an editor and installing a plugin for the Elm language

- Getting a first look at the Elm language

- Deciding how to deploy an Elm application

- Organizing the source code of an application for easier development

We will just handle the basics in this chapter; more advanced topics will be discussed in Chapter 4.

Installation

We have to install the Elm platform to get started. This does not mean that we have to install a runtime as in other systems like Java or .Net. The Elm platform is self-contained without runtime dependencies. Of course, since Elm compiles to JavaScript we will need a browser and a JavaScript engine to run the compiled Elm application.

To use the Elm platform, we just have to get the tools onto our computer that compile Elm code, install packages our code depends on, and run the compiled code on a development server.

13

© Wolfgang Loder 2018
W. Loder, *Web Applications with Elm*, https://doi.org/10.1007/978-1-4842-2610-0_2

Note   The Elm platform supports all *modern* browsers. It seems that there is no known lower bounds for Chrome, Firefox, Opera, or Safari, also helped by the effective update process of these browsers, which keeps the browsers and JavaScript engines on the latest version. Internet Explorer before version 9 does not work—but it can't be considered *modern*.

The Elm Guide[1] provides links to installers for Mac OS and Windows. Alternatively, it is possible to install the platform with npm. Node is a prerequisite to work with tools of the Elm platform, and npm[2] is installed together with Node,[3] which itself has several installation options on all major platforms. Most probably readers of this book have Node installed anyway.

The installation using npm is an operating system–independent way and is valid for Mac OS, Windows, and Linux. We will focus on this option in this book.

Note   Make sure that the node installation does not need elevated administrator rights to run (*su/sudo* on Mac or Linux); otherwise, you will get errors when running Elm platform tools.

Once npm is on the computer and verified to work we can install the Elm platform, either locally in a project or globally on the development computer. If we don't want to install the Elm platform on the physical machine at all, we can use a Docker image.

Tip   Another package manager is *yarn*,[4] which works with npm and other package formats and has some advanced features compared to npm. Some example projects in the downloadable source code use yarn, but throughout the book we will use only npm.

---

[1]https://guide.elm-lang.org/get_started.html
[2]https://docs.npmjs.com/
[3]https://nodejs.org/en/download/
[4]https://yarnpkg.com/

Global Installation

A global installation of the Elm platform can be done with the preceding mentioned installers, which you can download from the Elm website, but as mentioned before we are focusing on npm. The shell command shown in Listing 2-1 installs the Elm platform.

Listing 2-1. Install Elm with npm

```
$ npm install -g elm
```

The option -g tells npm to install the package globally. The Elm package we download from the npm repository is created during the publishing process of the Elm platform, so it will be up-to-date with the latest stable version and will have the same version as the operating system–specific installers.

After running the npm installation, we can check if the Elm platform is set up by simply running the command elm on the command line (Listing 2-2).

Listing 2-2. Run elm

```
$ elm
Elm Platform 0.18.0 - a way to run all Elm tools

Usage: elm <command> [<args>]

Available commands include:
  make      Compile an Elm file or project into JS or HTML
  package   Manage packages from <http://package.elm-lang.org>
  reactor   Develop with compile-on-refresh and time-travel debugging
  repl      A REPL for running individual expressions
```

The output of the command in the preceding listing has lines omitted for brevity, but we can see the most important information. The installed version of the Elm platform provides four commands. We will use all these commands in the following chapters, so we won't explain them in detail now. At this moment, we just want to make sure that the Elm platform is installed and can be run.

The caveat is that running the command elm does not prove that the Elm platform tools are actually working. The basic elm command calls other tools to do its tasks, so we need to call at least one other tool to make sure.

We can test our installation by calling the tool `elm-repl` from the command line. You can use either `elm repl` or `elm-repl`. The `elm` command with option `repl` calls the program with the dash in it. See Listing 2-3.

Listing 2-3. Run elm-repl

```
$ elm-repl
---- elm-repl 0.18.0 -----------------------------------------------------
 :help for help, :exit to exit, more at <https://github.com/elm-lang/elm-repl>
--------------------------------------------------------------------------
> _
```

If you see an output similar to that in the listing—your version number may be different—then your installation of the Elm platform was successful.

Tip   On some Linux systems you may get an error when running `elm-repl`. Most likely this has to do with a missing dependency called `libtinfo` that needs to be installed manually from the Linux distribution repository. On all Linux distributions the installed version of Node may not be the latest. If you get an error about "Haskell sandbox" or similar, upgrade to the latest Node version. For Elm version 0.18.x I have successfully used Node versions 6.9.x and 7.x.

With the installation finished and at least partially validated, we have the Elm platform available on our computer. Since this is a global installation we can run the command `elm` and the Elm platform tools from a command line in any directory on our computer.

Local Installation

The global installation of the Elm platform has its advantages, but it is not always the desired solution. Often, there is a need to install the Elm platform locally in a project. The platform is evolving rapidly, and changes from one version to the next may break the code of an existing application.

My own setup is to have the latest version globally installed; for example, the latest development version. For some projects, I can use a local version of the Elm platform or a Docker container.

Caution   If you use the installers from the Elm website, the Elm platform will always be installed globally.

To install the Elm platform in the directory of an Elm project, we can run the following command, which is similar to the global installation but without the -g flag (Listing 2-4).

Listing 2-4. Install Elm in a Project

```
npm install --save elm
```

This will install the Elm platform in the default directory for node packages, named node_modules, in the directory we ran the preceding command from. The directory node_modules will be created automatically if it does not yet exist, but you must have a file package.json with at least an empty root level (*{}*), otherwise npm fails with an error. The section dependencies will be updated with the Elm package dependency.

Instead of having the Elm platform as a normal dependency, it is better to indicate that it is only needed for development. See Listing 2-5.

Listing 2-5. Install Elm as dev Dependency

```
npm install --save-dev elm
```

The preceding command will add Elm to the section devDependencies. This is only important if the project source code is installed by other developers who do not want to have a local Elm version because their global version is correct. They can then use npm install -production to install only normal project dependencies.

Tip   The package manager yarn not only installs a package without the file package.json already created in the installation directory, but it also automatically creates this file and adds a dependency section with the installed Elm package as a dependency. The packages are installed as usual in the directory node_modules.

A local installation is not without problems if we also have a global Elm installation. For example, we can't type simply `elm`, because this would run the global version. We have to use the correct path for the desired Elm version. To help us type less, we can define scripts in `package.json` (see Listing 2-6).

Listing 2-6. Scripts in package.json

```
"scripts": {
  "c": "node_modules/.bin/elm make src/main.elm --output elm.js",
  "cw": "node_modules/.bin/elm make src/main.elm --output elm.js --warn",
  "r": "node_modules/.bin/elm repl"
}
```

With these few lines added, we can now invoke the command `npm run c` and it will compile the file `main.elm` using the local Elm version. Similarly, `npm run cw` will write out warnings when compiling, and `npm run r` will open the local `elm-repl`. These options will become clearer when we discuss the compilation and deployment of our projects later in this chapter.

Running a Docker Container

If we don't want to install the Elm platform on our computers, we could run a Docker container. The Docker system needs to be installed, but there are easy installation options for Mac OS,[5] Windows,[6] and Linux distributions; for example, Ubuntu.[7] The new installers for Mac OS and Windows have the advantage that no additional virtual-machine environment like VirtualBox needs to be installed and run. The needed virtual machines are included in the Docker installation.

On Docker Hub, several Elm containers can be found.[8] They can easily be downloaded and installed into the Docker system, but many developers like to have more control and want to create their own container configurations. Listing 2-7 shows a simple Dockerfile that creates a Docker image that runs the Elm platform.

---

[5]`https://docs.docker.com/engine/installation/mac/`
[6]`https://docs.docker.com/engine/installation/windows/`
[7]`https://docs.docker.com/engine/installation/linux/ubuntulinux/`
[8]`https://hub.docker.com/search/?i&page=1&q=elm`

Listing 2-7. Dockerfile Elm Image

```
FROM haskell:7.10.2
MAINTAINER Wolfgang Loder <wolfgang.loder@googlemail.com>
ENV ELM_VER=master

RUN apt-get update && apt-get install -y \
    curl \
    git \
    libtinfo-dev \
    nodejs
ENV PATH /opt/Elm-Platform/$ELM_VER/.cabal-sandbox/bin:$PATH
WORKDIR /opt
RUN curl \
 https://raw.githubusercontent.com/elm-lang/ \
 elm-platform/master/installers/BuildFromSource.hs
 > BuildFromSource.hs
RUN runhaskell BuildFromSource.hs $ELM_VER
EXPOSE 8000 8000
ENTRYPOINT ["elm"]
```

This image is based on the official Haskell image and builds the Elm platform, which is written in Haskell, from source code. The source can be found on GitHub,[9] and in this example we use the master branch, which is the latest version. It is also possible to define a specific version by supplying a tag like 0.17.0.

Note   For current Elm versions, the supported Haskell version is 7.10.2, which is not the latest version. If you previously installed a Haskell image in your Docker system before, it may be an incorrect version. So don't be surprised if the preceding Docker command downloads a nearly 1 GB file during the creation of the Elm platform image.

---

[9]https://github.com/elm-lang/elm-platform

With a working Docker installation on our computer, we can create our image. First, we need to open a command-line interface in the directory where our Dockerfile is saved. Then, we can run the following command, which will pick up the Dockerfile in the current directory; note the `dot` argument to indicate the directory (Listing 2-8).

Listing 2-8. Create Docker Container

```
docker build -t elmexposed:1.0 .
```

A new image called `elmexposed` with the tag `1.0` will be created. The name hints at the fact that it can be used like a global installation of the Elm platform, but it is not interactive in the sense that it provides a bash prompt.

The best way to invoke Elm commands in the container is to set an alias in the CLI with the `docker run` command. Another important startup option is to set a working directory on our machine to bind it to the container as well. In addition, we will expose a port from the container so we can test the Elm application. The following command, formatted for readability, sets the alias (Listing 2-9).

Listing 2-9. Run Docker Image

```
alias elmex='docker run
  -it
  -v $(pwd):/Hello-World
  -w /Hello-World
  -p 8000:8000
  -e "HOME=/tmp"
  --rm elmexposed:1.0'
```

We call the alias `elmex` so it does not interfere with the Elm installation on our computer. The directory of our example, `Hello-world`—see the downloadable code—is bound to the container and is used as the working directory. For this to work we have to run the command in the `Hello-world` directory to set `pwd` to the correct value.

When we run `elm reactor`, Docker will forward every response on port 8000 in the container to port 8000 on the computer that hosts the container. Vice versa, all requests on port 8000 on our computer will be forwarded to the container. In our browser, we will see the expected *Hello World* string displayed as if we were running `elm-reactor` on our physical computer.

It seems a little bit complicated to build the Elm platform from scratch when creating our elmexposed Docker image. Not only does it take some time, but the image itself is quite big.

There is a way to expose Elm by creating a Docker image via an npm installation, as we discussed before (Listing 2-10).

Listing 2-10. Dockerfile: Elm Installation with npm

```
FROM ubuntu:latest
MAINTAINER Wolfgang Loder <wolfgang.loder@googlemail.com>

RUN apt-get update && apt-get install -y \
  apt-utils \
  curl \
  git \
  libtinfo-dev \
  build-essential
RUN curl -sL https://deb.nodesource.com/setup_7.x | sudo -E bash -
RUN sudo apt-get install -y nodejs
RUN npm install -g elm
EXPOSE 8000 8000
```

This configuration uses the latest official Ubuntu distribution, installs Node, and installs the package elm with npm using the same command we discussed earlier. It also exposes port 8000 from the container.

As before, we create the image with docker build, and this time we give our image the name elminteractive (Listing 2-11).

Listing 2-11. Run Elm with Docker

```
docker build -t elminteractive:1.0.
```

The difference from elmexposed is that we can create an interactive container with this image and get a bash prompt (Listing 2-12).

Listing 2-12. Interactive Docker Elm Container

```
docker run -it elminteractive:1.0
```

Now we can run any valid command on the Ubuntu system container—for example, elm -version—to see if the Elm platform was successfully installed.

We can also create a container that is attached to a directory on our computer and use the Elm platform as if it were installed on our physical computer. Listing 2-13 shows a bash session compiling the *Hello World* example. We define the directory and the port when we start the docker image.

Listing 2-13. Interactive Docker Elm Container with Local Directory

```
$ docker run -it -p 8000:8000 -v $(pwd):/Hello-World elminteractive:1.0

root@30bf0211b4fd:/# ls
  Hello-World  bin  boot  dev  etc  home  lib  lib64  media  mnt  opt  proc
  root  run  sbin  srv  sys  tmp  usr  var
root@30bf0211b4fd:/# cd Hello-World
root@30bf0211b4fd:/Hello-World# ls
  StandaloneIndex.html  elm-package.json  elm-stuff  elm.js  helloworld.html
  helloworld.js  index.html  main.elm
root@30bf0211b4fd:/Hello-World# elm make main.elm --output helloworld.js
  Success! Compiled 37 modules.
  Successfully generated helloworld.js
root@30bf0211b4fd:/Hello-World# elm reactor -a 0.0.0.0
  elm-reactor 0.17.1
  Listening on http://0.0.0.0:8000/
^C
  Shutting down...
root@30bf0211b4fd:/Hello-World# exit
$ _
```

After running the docker run command in the Hello-World directory of our computer with the preceding options we get a bash prompt. With ls we list the directories and see that the Hello-World directory is available. Changing the directory into it and listing the files, we see all the files and directories right in the container bash prompt.

The next step is to compile main.elm with the usual make command. Then, we run elm-reactor. The option -a sets the server address. This may not be necessary, but Mac OS, which I used, does not recognize localhost when ports are exposed from a Docker container. This is why we set the address to 0.0.0.0. The port is the default port 8000 we exposed in the Dockerfile.

On our computer, we run http://0.0.0.0:8000/Hello-World/index.html and get the string *Hello World* rendered.

By creating Docker images and containers we can have several Elm platform versions on our computer without having to install anything globally or in a project. It is up to the developer as to which option is preferred. In the end, they all lead to having the Elm platform available for development.

Editors and IDEs

No matter which option we choose for installing the Elm platform, we will need an editor or an IDE to write code.

Developers working with Java Virtual Machine or .Net languages are used to IDEs with extensive support for various development tasks, such as the following:

- Intellisense

- Autocompletion

- Refactoring, like changing symbol names

- Jumping to definitions and symbols

- Formatting code

- Debugging support

- Integration of tools

Newer languages like Elixir or Elm do not provide the luxury of a full-blown IDE, but there are plugins for editors available that achieve some of the tasks just listed. The following sections list some of the most popular editors and their plugin options.

Tip   Before installing a plugin you should check if it can handle the Elm platform version you are running.

The following list is in alphabetical order, not in order of preference.

Atom

There are quite a few plugins available for Atom that target the Elm platform. The one listed here incorporates other plugins for a complete experience.

- Plugin Name: `Elmjutsu`

- Link: `atom.io/packages/elmjutsu`

- Features: syntax highlighting, autocomplete, go to (definition, symbol, usage), rename (symbol)

- Comments: This plugin helps with writing code only; it does not have an integration with the Elm platform tools.

Emacs

The listed plugin is the only one at the moment supporting Elm. There is a `FlyCheck` support for Elm available (`github.com/bsermons/flycheck-elm`), but it has not been updated for a while, so it does not support the latest language version at the time of writing.

- Plugin Name: `elm-mode`

- Link: `github.com/jcollard/elm-mode`

- Features: syntax highlighting, autocomplete (via `elm-oracle` and company), intelligent indentation, integration with Elm platform tools and `elm-format`.

IntelliJ

The plugin works with IntelliJ Community Edition and other IDEs.

- Plugin Name: `elm-plugin`

- Link: `plugins.jetbrains.com/plugin/8192`

- Features: syntax highlighting, autocomplete, syntax parser, go to (declaration), rename refactoring, brace matching, highlighting unresolved references, spellchecking.

LightTable

LightTable is an editor that is not used as often as others in this list, but the plugin described here is one of the best I have experienced.

- Plugin Name: elm-light
- Link: github.com/rundis/elm-light
- Features: syntax highlighting, autocomplete, linting and for some errors, inline docs, find usages, module browser, go to (definition), integration with elm-repo, elm-reactor, and elm-format
- Comments: Extensive manual available at rundis.gitbooks.io/ elm-light-guide/content/.

Sublime

This plugin is compatible with sublime 2 and 3.

- Plugin Name: Elm Package Support
- Link: packagecontrol.io/packages/Elm%20Language%20Support
- Features: syntax highlighting, autocomplete, integration with elm-repl and elm-make
- Comments: The integration with elm-repo requires the installation of another plugin (SublimeREPL).

Vim

The plugin has very good integration with the Elm platform tools and includes an option to run unit tests from within the editor.

- Plugin Name: elm-vim
- Link: github.com/ElmCast/elm-vim
- Features: syntax highlighting, autocomplete, automatic indentation, linting, integration with elm-repl, elm-make, elm-format, and elm-test.

Visual Studio Code

The plugin is under active development and intends to add features like refactoring.

- Plugin Name: `elm`

- Link: `github.com/sbrink/vscode-elm`

- Features: syntax highlighting, autocomplete, error highlighting, function information, integration with `elm-repl`, `elm-reactor`, and `elm-format`

Note   In this and the following chapters I will not refer to specific editor plugins, but I will use a CLI to invoke commands.

The editor support for the Elm platform is not yet great, but it is improving steadily. Which editor you use depends on your individual preferences. Also, editor performance and feature sets change over time, and it makes sense to retry editors even when you have rejected them previously.

Obligatory *Hello World*

After installing the Elm platform and deciding on an editor, we are ready to write a first Elm program. As is tradition, we have to implement a *Hello World* program in Elm. Let's do this now to test the Elm platform installation and our editors.

Create a directory called `Hello-World` on your computer and then create a file with the name `main.elm`. Insert the statements shown in Listing 2-14.

Listing 2-14. Hello World in Elm

```elm
module Hello exposing (..)

import Html exposing (text)

main : Html.Html msg
main =
    text "Hello World"
```

These few lines of code will render *Hello World,* which is achieved with the line text "Hello World". The word text refers to a function of the same name in the package Html. We don't care at this moment what text will be compiled into, we just know that the argument *Hello World* will be printed on the web page. Presumably the compilation will result in a span tag or similar.

The first line of the code defines a module with the name Hello that exports (*exposes*) all the functions defined in the module. The import statement tells the compiler that we want to use the text function from the module Html. The line main: Html.Html msg is a type annotation and explains which types the arguments and return result of the function main are.

This code will be much clearer after working through the next two chapters, where we will get to know Elm as a language and a platform.

Note   *Compiler* or *transpiler*? Both terms refer to transforming one language into another language. Which term to use depends on the similarity of the two languages. For example, transforming TypeScript into JavaScript is usually seen as transpiling because the two languages are very close to each other and JavaScript can even be mixed with TypeScript in the same file. We could discuss whether Elm is significantly different from JavaScript or not. Many including myself believe it is, so we are using the term *compiling* throughout the book when we mean transforming Elm into JavaScript.

The next step is to compile the Elm program into JavaScript. We open a command line in the Hello-World directory and run the command shown in Listing 2-15, assuming that we are using a global installation of Elm.

Listing 2-15. Run elm-make

```
$ elm-make main.elm
  Some new packages are needed. Here is the upgrade plan.
    Install:
      elm-lang/core 4.0.5
      elm-lang/html 1.1.0
      elm-lang/virtual-dom 1.1.1
```

```
Do you approve of this plan? [Y/n]
Starting downloads...
  - elm-lang/virtual-dom 1.1.1
  - elm-lang/html 1.1.0
  - elm-lang/core 4.0.5
Packages configured successfully!
Success! Compiled 31 modules.
Successfully generated index.html
```

This simple command is doing a lot of work in the background. We just ask to make a JavaScript version of the file main.elm, but other tasks need to be done first before the code can be compiled.

The first time that elm-make runs it will generate a generic elm-package.json file if it does not yet exist and then ask if we are happy to download a few Elm packages. These packages will be copied into a directory created by elm-make with the name elm-stuff and then be compiled. Then, main.elm will be compiled as well, and a file index.html will be generated.

The elm-package.json file is similar to the package.json file we use with Node. It lists the dependencies we have in our project and a few other key–value pairs to define information about the project. See Listing 2-16.

Listing 2-16. Generated elm-package.json

```
{
    "version": "1.0.0",
    "summary": "helpful summary of your project, less than 80 characters",
    "repository": "https://github.com/user/project.git",
    "license": "BSD3",
    "source-directories": [
        "."
    ],
    "exposed-modules": [],
    "dependencies": {
        "elm-lang/core": "5.0.0 <= v < 6.0.0",
        "elm-lang/html": "2.0.0 <= v < 3.0.0"
    },
    "elm-version": "0.18.0 <= v < 0.19.0"
}
```

The directory elm-stuff (Figure 2-1) contains both compiled packages (packages) and all the files created during compilation (build-artifacts).

Figure 2-1. *Directory elm-stuff*

There is also an exact-dependencies file in the elm-stuff directory that lists all the packages with names and versions that were downloaded during the make process.

> **Tip**   If you get strange errors during compilation that you can't explain, it usually
> helps to delete the directory `elm-stuff` and run make again. It will re-create all
> packages, and then the compilation will most probably succeed.

After successful compilation we are now ready to launch the application with
elm-reactor (Listing 2-17).

Listing 2-17. Run elm-reactor

```
$ elm-reactor
  elm-reactor 0.18.0
  Listening on http://localhost:8000/
```

A local server will start at port 8000, and opening the URL `http://localhost:8000/`
`index.html` in a browser will display *Hello World*.

Now we know not only that Elm is installed on our machine, but also that Elm files
compile and run in a browser.

Deployment

Once an application has been implemented, compiled, and—in our simple example—
manually tested in `elm-reactor`, it is time to deploy the compiled Elm application to a
web server. There are three options available to us.

Option 1: All-in-One

This is the standard option, which we used in the *Hello World* example. By default,
`elm-make` takes the name of the Elm source-code file to be compiled and does not need
any other arguments. A file with the default name `index.html` will be created with our
compiled source code.

Our *Hello World* program is only a few lines of Elm code, but the created HTML file
has more than 7900 lines and a size of 183 KB. This seems like a lot, but we need to keep
in mind that each compiled Elm program is running on top of a runtime that includes
code for any package we use.

Note   At the moment, the Elm compiler does not offer *tree-shaking* to remove not-needed code or dead code. It may be implemented in future versions of the Elm platform.

Looking at index.html reveals that the last line is the important and only markup (Listing 2-18).

Listing 2-18. Generated index.html (excerpt)

```
  </script>
 </head>
 <body>
   <script type="text/javascript">Elm.Hello.fullscreen()</script>
 </body>
</html>
```

We do not print the whole file, so the first lines in the listing close any open HTML tags. In the body tag, a script is defined that calls our Elm module Hello. All the lines before are necessary to make this simple call happen and are pure JavaScript. They define an object Elm that knows our module as object Hello (remember our module definition), which defines several functions, among them fullscreen(). The object Elm was created during compilation of the Elm code.

Calling elm-make without additional arguments besides the code file gets us started, but no further. If we don't like the name index.html we can call elm-make in such a way that the HTML file is created with a different name (Listing 2-19).

Listing 2-19. Create Custom Name HTML File

```
elm-make main.elm --output helloworld.html
```

This command will create the file helloworld.html. This changes the name only; the content is the same as in the previous index.html.

Most probably you want to link to your CSS files or just embed the Elm application into an existing web page. This is what Option 2 is for.

Option 2: Custom Web Page

We start by creating a JavaScript file instead of an HTML page. The command is similar to the previous elm-make command, only the output flag is set to a file with the suffix js (Listing 2-20).

Listing 2-20. Make JavaScript File

```
elm-make main.elm --output helloworld.js
```

The output of this command is a JavaScript file with the name helloworld.js. The big difference from the HTML file is that it does not have any markup; it is a JavaScript file, after all.

The advantage of creating a JavaScript file is that we can now link to it from any HTML file. A basic markup example to do this is shown in Listing 2-21.

Listing 2-21. Standalone HTML Page

```
<!DOCTYPE html>
<html>
  <head>
  </head>
  <body>
    <script>
      if (typeof module === 'object') {
        window.module = module; module = undefined;
      }
    </script>
    <script src="./helloworld.js"></script>
    <script>if (window.module) module = window.module;</script>
    <script type="text/javascript">Elm.Hello.fullscreen()</script>
  </body>
</html>
```

The way to link to helloworld.js is a bit unusual. A normal link in the header would suffice for now, but this way works both in browsers and with module systems like CommonJS.

Another advantage of creating a JavaScript file and linking to it is that we can minify the resulting JavaScript code. Google's Closure Compiler[10] is a Java executable that can be used from the command line. The zipped download has an executable with a long name that includes version and date information, so we renamed the file to cc.jar. The command in Listing 2-22 assumes that the compiler (cc.jar) can be accessed from anywhere and that we are in the directory of the *AllBasics* example.

Listing 2-22. Closure Compiler

```
$ java -jar cc.jar --js allbasics.js \
    > /tmp/elm.js && mv /tmp/elm.js elm.js
```

We define elm.js as an input file, and after minification we overwrite it with the same name. The result is that the file size shrinks from 76 KB to 26 KB. You may get a warning about unreachable code. Other experiments with the closure compiler achieved file-size shrinks from 183 KB to 62 KB when, for example, the HTML package was imported.

Note   Not every JavaScript file created by the Elm compiler can be used with the closure compiler, and you might get errors. The method to analyze the JavaScript code is only a workaround. The next versions of Elm will have tree shaking—the removal of unused code, especially in libraries—built into the Elm compiler.

We can run our custom page with either the minified or the not minified JavaScript file and get the same result, as expected. The statement Elm.Hello.fullscreen() still expands the Elm application across the full width of our browser window.

What happens if we want to use our Elm application only in a part of our page, not fullscreen? We simply use Option 3.

Option 3: Integration

The previous two options saw a JavaScript file created and linked to from a custom HTML page. Now, we want to take the *Hello World* application, which is just a short text, and display it in a div element on our custom page.

---

[10]https://developers.google.com/closure/compiler/

The following simple web page links to the JavaScript we create with elm-make, but attaches it to an HTML element, in our case a div (see Listing 2-23).

Listing 2-23. Embedded Elm Application

```
<!DOCTYPE html>
<html>
  <head>
  </head>
  <body>
    <script>
      if (typeof module === 'object')
        {window.module = module; module = undefined;}
    </script>
    <script src="./elm.js"></script>
    <script>if (window.module) module = window.module;</script>
    <div>
      Element before the embedded Elm app
    </div>
    <div id="elm-main"></div>
    <div>
      Element after the embedded Elm app
    </div>
    <script>
      var elmDiv = document.getElementById('elm-main');
      var elmApp = Elm.Hello.embed(elmDiv)
    </script>
  </body>
</html>
```

The script sections to link to elm.js are the same as before. The embedding happens in the script section after we have defined some div tags. One of those has the ID elm-main, and so we search for the element with that ID. Then, we call the function Elm.Hello.embed(elmDiv) with the DOM element reference of the div with the ID elm-main as argument.

Instead of the function fullscreen we call the function embed, which is defined in JavaScript in the object Hello.

We save the HTML file with the name embedded.html in the directory Hello-World and can test it with elm-reactor. The browser will render what is shown in Figure 2-2.

Element before the embedded Elm app
Hello World
Element after the embedded Elm app

Figure 2-2. *Embedded Elm application*

As expected, all the div tags are rendered, and the embedded Hello module displays *Hello World* in the tag we defined.

Embedding compiled Elm modules opens up opportunities to introduce Elm slowly into existing web applications. The same module can be integrated several times, or several modules can be integrated on one or more pages.

Note   If we embed a module more than once then it will always include the Elm runtime in the module. At the moment, there is no official way to link to the Elm runtime only once.

What We Have Learned

This chapter got us set up with the following:

- We have the Elm platform installed, either on our computer or run as a Docker container.

- Our preferred editor has a plugin to make coding with the Elm language easier.

- We saw a simple *Hello World* program and learned how to compile it and test it in the browser with the built-in server.

- At the end of the chapter, we saw different ways to integrate a compiled Elm project into a web application.

In the next chapter, we will finally learn the Elm language.

CHAPTER 3

Elm Primer

In the first chapter, we saw several Elm application examples. This chapter will provide a deeper look into Elm and is all about the language and standard libraries.

I recommend you read this chapter in sequence because the language explanations build from easier features to more advanced features.

Elm Platform

Elm is not only a language, but also a platform with which to create web applications. It has tools and a runtime that is necessary in order to run an Elm application derived from Elm code. When we compile even a small application like the *Hello World* example from Chapter 2, the Elm compiler creates a JavaScript file with the code of the application, and it also integrates needed runtime functions and any other library code that is used. For example, it includes the Html package that has, among others, a function text to display text on a web page.

Tip   As mentioned before, the Elm platform is written in Haskell, with occasional part implementations in Elm. All source code can be found on GitHub.[1] It is not necessary to understand the Haskell code, but it may be of interest to see what is behind the Elm platform surface.

We already encountered elm-make in Chapter 2 when we created a simple *Hello World* program. When we run the command elm make it will call internally elm-make to create an executable form of a project. *Executable* in this context means a JavaScript file that can be interpreted by a JavaScript engine.

---

[1]https://github.com/elm-lang

© Wolfgang Loder 2018
W. Loder, *Web Applications with Elm*, https://doi.org/10.1007/978-1-4842-2610-0_3

As the name *make* suggests, the tool does more than just compile. It also checks the validity of the configurations in `elm-package.json` and the status of packages. With several command-line arguments available, `elm make` can be configured at runtime for various scenarios.

The following overview lists the other tools of the Elm platform that help with the development process:

- `elm-package` — This is Elm's package manager, similar to npm. The Elm platform maintains a package repository.[2] At the moment, the tool can't handle local packages, which is one of the reasons one can find packages that are out of date or unfinished. This will hopefully change in the future. In the meantime, there are workarounds available to trick Elm into believing that a package was downloaded by manipulating files in the directory `elm-stuff`. Overall, the package manager works as expected and handles version problems well. For example, if there is no version of a package matching the used Elm language version, `elm-package` will throw an error.

- `elm-reactor` — This is an interactive web application that can run and compile Elm code. It has debug options that have changed over time. During development it is not always necessary to run the `elm-reactor`, because the compiled code is just JavaScript, which can be embedded in any HTML page and run on any local server—or even in the browser from a file if it is run in such a way that browser restrictions do not kick in.

- `elm-repl` — This is the *read–eval–print loop* tool that allows interactive programming. It is perfect for trying small examples and has some configuration options.

Elm Style Guide

The creator of Elm is very clear about how he envisions Elm code should be written. It may not be what you are used to from other languages or would like yourself, but a consistent coding style makes it easier to read code from somebody else or to maintain

---

[2]`http://package.elm-lang.org/`

code later. To make this task easier, we want to format our code while writing it without thinking too much about the intricacies of the formatting rules. The style guide can be found on the Elm website,[3] and discussions about it can be found in the Discourse group *Elm Discuss*.[4]

Some editors with Elm plugins, as discussed in Chapter 2, may have code formatting already built in. Most of them rely on `elm-format`,[5] which can also be run from the command line. If you don't want the integration in an editor, you can install `elm-format` locally in a project. The plugins can format the code either when saving or on demand, but not all common editors support all options. The *elm-format* GitHub website has a table with information about editor integrations and installation instructions.

The formatting tool is in *alpha*, and at the time of writing there are issues open that may make the formatting fail or format in a way you don't want. When you find an issue, just report it—there are many contributors working on this project, and the issue will likely be resolved in the next release. The tool can be built from source as well, but you will need to have a working Haskell installation on your computer.

Tip   By default, the formatting tool overwrites the source code file if you answer *yes* when prompted, so be careful and check the formatted output or invoke it with the option `--output FILE`. The argument `FILE` gives the name of a file the formatted code should be written to. Another useful option is `--elm-version VERSION` to define the version of the platform the code file is supposed to support. There is also the option `--stdin`, which reads from the stdin device and outputs on the stdout device.

Have a look at the following Elm code (Listing 3-1). It is not formatted in a particular way, but rather written in a way that developers coming from other languages may prefer or in their own individual style.

---

[3]http://elm-lang.org/docs/style-guide
[4]https://discourse.elm-lang.org
[5]https://github.com/avh4/elm-format

> **Note**   The code in the listing compiles but does not make much sense otherwise; for example, the functions `update` and `view` are not hit. This example's sole purpose is to show formatting for different language features.

Listing 3-1. Non-formatted Source Code

```
module Hello exposing (..)
import Html exposing (div, input, text, form, button)
import Html.Events exposing (onClick, onInput)
import String

type Msg = Change String | Check | Suggest (List String)

main =
  text "Hello World"

update msg model =
  case msg of
    Change m -> ( m, Cmd.none )
    _ -> ("", Cmd.none)

view model =
  div [][ input [ onInput Change ] [],
    button [ onClick Check ] [ text "Check" ],
    div [] [ text (String.join ", " model.suggestions) ]
  ]
```

We run `elm-format` in a shell with the command `elm-format main.elm --yes`, assuming that our code file is saved in the current directory, has the name `main.elm`, and `elm-format` was installed globally. The option `--yes` means that we say automatically *yes* to all prompts.

The formatting tool will run and—in our case—will overwrite `main.elm` with the formatted version. To create a file without overwriting the original file we could invoke the command `elm-format main.elm --output formatted.elm`. This will create the file `formatted.elm` in the current directory.

Let's have a look at the formatted file in Listing 3-2.

Listing 3-2. Formatted Source Code

```
module Hello exposing (..)

import Html exposing (div, input, text, form, button)
import Html.Events exposing (onClick, onInput)
import String

type Msg
    = Change String
    | Check
    | Suggest (List String)

main =
    text "Hello World"

update msg model =
    case msg of
        Change m ->
            ( m, Cmd.none )

        _ ->
            ( "", Cmd.none )

view model =
    div []
        [ input [ onInput Change ] []
        , button [ onClick Check ] [ text "Check" ]
        , div [] [ text (String.join ", " model.suggestions) ]
        ]
```

Immediately, we notice that the line number has increased by 50 percent. Between declarations are two empty lines; also, statements in the case expression are separated by one empty line. The most controversial rule of the guideline is the formatting of the function view. The *leading comma* style is unusual for developers coming from C#, Java, or even JavaScript, although there are discussions in the Node.js and JavaScript community to introduce this style. For Haskell developers this style is not unusual and is used to separate list and similar items.

Elm's style rules are based on easier maintenance, easy readability, and clean diffs. In this book we adhere to the style guide except for deleting additional empty lines or formatting code to keep it compact for easier reading.

Elm Language

Elm as a language can be seen from different angles. The main purpose of the language and the platform is to create web applications. Elm is not a general-purpose language, and it is difficult and sometimes impossible to break out of the web constraints.

In general, we can define Elm as shown in Figure 3-1.

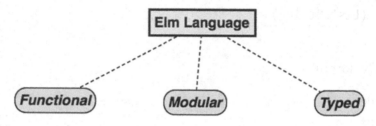

Figure 3-1. *Elm language*

Elm is a functional, typed, and modular language. In addition to these points, Elm has basic features, like other languages have, that make it possible to write expressions or control the program flow. Some parts of the language as discussed here are defined in Haskell code to define the structure of the language. Other parts are written in Elm itself and can be found in the core library.[6] Additional types and functionality are found in library modules that can be imported as needed. The core library is automatically loaded and is part of the JavaScript runtime that is created during compilation.

Note   This chapter is based on Elm version 0.18, which introduced a few breaking changes compared to previous versions. Example code on websites or blog posts can be outdated if not updated to the latest version, and the syntax may differ from the examples in this book.

---

[6]https://github.com/elm-lang/core

In the following pages, we will use the preceding classification—functional, modular, typed—to give an overview of the language.

Code examples are either taken from a code module called `AllBasics.elm` or were directly edited in `elm-repl`. All `repl` lines starting with `>` are input, and the output is formatted with an indentation to make it easier to read. The module `AllBasics` is in the source code in the directory `Basics`.

Basic Language Features

The basic language features in Elm provide ways to express operations on values using operators and control how these expressions are integrated in the statement flow of an implementation.

Note Many of the following examples need the example Elm file called `allbasics.elm` that is provided with this book. To use functions and types in that file, navigate to its location, run `elm repl`, and then in the REPL type `import AllBasics exposing (..)`. Missing libraries will be downloaded, and then the Elm code will be compiled into a temporary JavaScript file.

Operators

The Elm language provides operators we are used to from other languages. It also has some more unconventional operators, at least if you are not familiar with Haskell.

Arithmetic Operators

Arithmetic operators work with numeric values and return a numeric value. They are all binary and take two operands. See Listing 3-3.

Listing 3-3. Arithmetic Operators

```
> 1.0 + 2        -- addition
  3 : Float
> 2 - 1.0        -- subtraction
  1 : Float
```

```
> 1 * 3.1 * 2  -- multiplication
  6.2 : Float
> 6.0 / 2       -- floating-point division
  3 : Float
> 4 / 2         -- floating-point division
  2 : Float
> 3 // 2        -- integer division
  1 : Int
> 2 ^ 8         -- exponentiation
  256 : number
> 3 % 2         -- modulo
  1 : Int
```

The arithmetic operators take either an integer or a float, except for the specialized division operators for float and integer and the modulo operator, which only makes sense with integer values.

The floating-point division will always return a float value, no matter which type the operands are. The integer division discards the remainder as expected, but the similarity of the operators / and // may lead to unexpected behavior if the developer is not careful.

Bitwise Operators

Bitwise operators take two integer values and return an integer value. See Listing 3-4.

Listing 3-4. Bitwise Operators

```
> import Bitwise exposing (..)
> and 255 128  -- bitwise and
  128 : Int
> or 255 128   -- bitwise or
  255 : Int
> Bitwise.xor 255 128  -- bitwise xor
  127 : Int
```

The calling of bitwise operators is different than we have seen with the arithmetic operator examples. They are both functions, but one is called *infix*, the other one *prefix*. We will look at the differences and declaration options for each later in this chapter.

If you try the examples in elm-repl you have to import the module Bitwise first. Still, the operator xor has a name conflict with a function of the same name in the module Basics, so we have to call xor fully qualified with the module name prefixed.

Logical Operators

Logical operators take two Boolean arguments and return a Boolean result. See Listing 3-5.

Listing 3-5. Logical Operators

```
> p1 = Calzone
  Calzone : AllBasics.Pizza
> p2 = Margherita
  Margherita : AllBasics.Pizza

> p1 == QuattroStagione && p2 == Margherita
  False : Bool
> p1 == Calzone && p2 == Margherita
  True : Bool
> p1 == QuattroStagione || p2 == Margherita
  True : Bool
> p1 == Calzone || p2 == Margherita
  True : Bool
> not (p1 == Calzone) && p2 == Margherita
  False : Bool
> not (p1 == Calzone) || p2 == Margherita
  True : Bool
```

These operators should not be mixed up with the bitwise operators, especially coming from other languages, where, for example, the word *and* is used for logical comparisons.

Comparison Operators

Comparison operators take two *comparable* types and return a Boolean value. We will discuss comparable types later in this chapter. Basically, they are standard number and string types on their own or in lists and tuples. See Listing 3-6.

Listing 3-6. Comparison Operators

```
> p1 = "Calzone"
  "Calzone" : String
> p2 = "Margherita"
  "Margherita" : String

> p1 == "Calzone"
  True : Bool
> p1 /= "Calzone"
  False : Bool
> p1 < p2
  True : Bool
> p1 <= p2
  True : Bool
> p1 > p2
  False : Bool
> p1 >= p2
  False : Bool
```

Comparisons work as in other languages. The notion of *comparable* in Elm is not yet fixed, so it may be possible that custom types can be made comparable in the future.

Functional Operators

Functional operators will become relevant when we discuss functions. They are used to pipe or compose functions. Listing 3-7 defines two functions for multiplying and adding numbers. We want to combine calls of these functions for given arguments and use *pipe operators*.

Listing 3-7. Pipe Operators

```
-- AllBasics
addNumbers : List number -> number
addNumbers list =
  List.foldr (+) 0 list

multiplyNumbers : number -> number -> number
multiplyNumbers value multiplicator =
  value * multiplicator
```

```
-- elm-repl
import AllBasics exposing (..)
> addNumbers [1,2] |> multiplyNumbers 3
  9 : number
> multiplyNumbers 3 <| addNumbers [1,2]
  9 : number
```

The first example uses the forwarding pipe operator. First, we calculate the addition—in our example, adding number items of a list—and then we pass the result to the function multiplyNumbers as the first argument. The functions will be evaluated from left to right.

The second example in the listing does the same thing, but by using the backward pipe operator the functions will be evaluated from right to left. The usage of any of these operators leads to the same result.

Composition operators work in a different way, but achieve similar results. See Listing 3-8.

Listing 3-8. Composition Operators

```
-- allbasics.elm
addNumbers : List number -> number
addNumbers list =
  List.foldr (+) 0 list

multiplyNumbers : number -> number -> number
multiplyNumbers value multiplicator =
  value * multiplicator

-- elm-repl
> fleft = addNumbers >> multiplyNumbers
  <function:_user$project$Repl$fleft> : List number -> number -> number
> fleft [1,2,3] 2
  12 : number
> fright = multiplyNumbers << addNumbers
  <function:_user$project$Repl$fright> : List number -> number -> number
> fright [1,2,3] 2
  12 : number
```

The type annotations give a hint of what is happening. The original function addNumbers takes a list of numbers and returns a number. The original function multiplyNumbers takes two numbers and returns the result as a number.

When we use the composition operators >> or << we *compose* a new function that takes a list of numbers and another number as the multiplier and delivers the result as a number.

Again, we can compose from the left or from the right; the resulting function has the same signature.

Special Operators

Another operator is the *concatenation operator* ::. Its purpose is to add elements to a list. See Listing 3-9.

Listing 3-9. Concatenation

```
type Pizza = Calzone | Margherita | QuattroStagione

addPizza : List Pizza -> Pizza -> List Pizza
addPizza l p =
  p :: l

firstPizza : List Pizza -> Maybe Pizza
firstPizza l =
  case l of
    head :: tail ->
      Just head
    [] -> Nothing

> firstPizza []
  Nothing : Maybe.Maybe AllBasics.Pizza
> firstPizza <| addPizza [Margherita] Calzone
  Just Calzone : Maybe.Maybe AllBasics.Pizza
> firstPizza [Margherita]
  Just Margherita : Maybe.Maybe AllBasics.Pizza
```

The function `addPizza` takes a list and an element and adds it as the first element. With the piping operator we can then send the resulting list to the function `firstPizza`. It uses `Maybe`—see later—to return either *Nothing* in case the list is empty or the first element of the list.

The `::` in the case expression pattern matches the `list` argument. If there is at least one element, `head` will return this element, and `tail` is the rest of the list, but it can also be empty if there is only one element.

The operator `++` concatenates two arguments if they are *appendable*; see later in the chapter when we discuss types to see what *appendable* means in Elm. See Listing 3-10.

Listing 3-10. Add to List

```
addPizzaOrdered : List Pizza -> List Pizza -> List Pizza
addPizzaOrdered l p =
  l ++ p

> addPizzaOrdered [Margherita] [Calzone]
  [Margherita,Calzone] : List AllBasics.Pizza
```

The function `addPizzaOrdered` simply adds two lists and returns one list with all elements of those two initial lists.

Control Structures

We need some structures to control the flow of statements in functions. In fact, there are only three control structures. You may miss `for` or `while`. As in other functional languages, these are expressed with recursive functions.

If

The `if` statement takes expressions that return a Boolean value and branches into statements depending on that value. These expressions can only evaluate to *True* or *False*; Elm does not have the notion of "truthiness."[7] See Listing 3-11.

---

[7]https://en.wikipedia.org/wiki/Truthiness

Listing 3-11. If

```
type Pizza = Calzone | Margherita | QuattroStagione

choosePizzaIf : Pizza -> String
choosePizzaIf p =
  if p == Calzone then
    "Pizza chosen: " ++ toString p
  else if p == Margherita then
    "Pizza chosen: " ++ toString p
  else
    "We don't serve this pizza"
```

This example has three branches and prints out the argument value. We see here the ++ operator again, which is used to concatenate two strings. We have a final else branch, which looks to be unnecessary. Let's omit it, compile again, and see what happens. See Listing 3-12.

Listing 3-12. If without else

```
choosePizzaIf p =
  if p == Calzone then
    "Pizza chosen: " ++ toString p
  else if p == Margherita then
    "Pizza chosen: " ++ toString p
```

To our surprise, we get an error. Normally, Elm compiler messages are quite useful, but in this case it is not clear at first glance what is needed. The clue lies in the phrase *You are missing some stuff.* It is the else branch that is needed. Every if needs an else. See Listing 3-13.

Listing 3-13. If Syntax Error

```
-- SYNTAX PROBLEM ------------------------------------------ allbasics.elm
```

I need whitespace, but got stuck on what looks like a new declaration. You are either missing some stuff in the declaration above or just need to add some spaces here:

```
I am looking for one of the following things:
    whitespace
Detected errors in 1 module.
```

The if control structure is not so much used in normal named functions, but more in anonymous functions.

Case

The case statement is the bread and butter of programming in Elm and other functional languages. It relies on pattern matching to determine which expression to evaluate.

The following example (Listing 3-14) does exactly the same thing as what the first (Listing 3-11) if example does.

Listing 3-14. Case

```
type Pizza = Calzone | Margherita | QuattroStagione

choosePizza : Pizza -> String
choosePizza p =
  case p of
    Calzone
      -> "Pizza chosen: " ++ toString p
    Margherita
      -> "Pizza chosen: " ++ toString p
    _
      -> "We don't serve this pizza"
```

We also see that all possible patterns need to be covered, similar to if-else. If we do not provide the last pattern with the underscore _, the compiler will complain. The underscore is a wildcard in this case and means that all other patterns should match this condition.

The case structure is used in many examples; you will encounter it often.

Let-In

The Let-In structure can be compared to assignment statements. The following very simple function returns a tuple. See Listing 3-15.

Listing 3-15. Let-In

```
type Pizza = Calzone | Margherita | QuattroStagione

pizzaOrders : ( Pizza, number )
pizzaOrders =
    let
      p = Calzone
      n = 5
    in
      (p,n)
```

The values for the returned tuple are calculated in the function. The let is like a block for defining local variables that can then be used in in.

Note   As with the other structures discussed in this chapter, let–in is an expression and can be used in any place expressions are allowed. In Elm we use a programming style that constructs bigger expressions from smaller expressions. Almost every function is then built from a big expression. Exceptions are, for example, constant functions.

Prefix and Infix Operators

We have seen that some operators can be called like we are used to in mathematics. Others have to be called like a function.

They are both functions, of course, but they are implemented in different ways; for example, the arithmetic operator + (Listing 3-16).

Listing 3-16. Arithmetic Operator +

```
-- AllBasics.elm
(+) : number -> number -> number
(+) =
  Native.Basics.add
```

We see that the function is declared as (+). This means that it can be used with an infix call, but can also be called as a normal function. See Listing 3-17.

Listing 3-17. Call Arithmetic Operator +

```
> 1 + 2.0       -- infix
  3 : Float
> (+) 1 2.0     -- prefix
  3 : Float
```

First, we call the + operator as an infix operator. Then, we call + in a prefix way. The function name is (+) in this case; the arguments are passed after the name, and the result is the same as in the infix case.

Note The use of infix operators with this syntax comes from Haskell. You can read more about the pros and cons in the Haskell wiki.[8]

We can define our own infix functions as well. It is not recommended to define new operators for public packages, but it is possible (Listing 3-18).

Listing 3-18. New Infix Operator

```
(++*) : List number -> number -> number
(++*) l m =
  case l of
    [] -> 0
    _ -> List.foldr (+) 0 l * m
```

This cryptic-looking function takes a list of numbers and a multiplier. It then calls List.foldr (+) 0 l, which adds all the numbers in the list. The result will be multiplied by the multiplier. The first line is a type annotation, and we will look at this a little bit later in this chapter. In Chapter 4 we will look at library modules like List.

We can call our new operator in two ways, as we saw with the + operator. See Listing 3-19.

---

[8]https://wiki.haskell.org/Use_of_infix_operators

Listing 3-19. Call New Infix Operator

```
> import AllBasics exposing (..)
> (++*) [1,2] 3
9 : number
> [1,2] ++* 3
9 : number
```

Both calls work as expected and yield the same result with the same arguments. The import on the first line is necessary to tell elm-repl where the new operator is defined.

Note   In previous versions of Elm it was possible to use backticks to call any binary function infix; for example, 1 `anybinfunc` 2. This functionality was replaced by using other operators or making an ordinary function call.

Elm as a Functional Language

The definition of a functional language is hard to pin down. Many times, discussions about this will involve arguments about pure and impure. Often, functional languages may have features of other paradigms embedded. For example, Scala and F# are certainly considered functional languages, but they also allow imperative or object-oriented constructs.

What we can say for sure is that the main feature of a functional language is that functions are first-class citizens. A function can be seen in mathematical terms as a map of input values to output values; it has no other effects than this mapping. When we call such a function we know that nothing else happens to any data outside of this function.

As we have mentioned, Elm is rooted in Haskell, so it is no surprise that Elm is a functional language with all the features normally associated with the functional paradigm.

Functions

The basis of Elm applications are functions, and almost everything is a function. We will see that even types define functions—in that case, *constructors*.

We have already seen simple function definitions and have used functions when we looked at operators. Roughly, functions can be divided into named and anonymous types.

Named Functions

Named functions are defined with a name that can be used to later call it (Listing 3-20).

Listing 3-20. Named Function

```
readMarkdownFile name =
    getChapter name
```

This function with the name `readMarkdownFile` has one parameter and calls in its body another function (`getChapter`) with the argument it was passed. Both functions are named and can be called from any module that knows about the functions.

The declaration of a function is similar to in other languages (Figure 3-2).

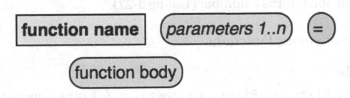

Figure 3-2. *Function declaration*

Function names start with a lowercase character and then usually continue with camel case, as in the example `readMarkdownFile`. Parameters are optional, but if used they have names starting with a lowercase character. The keyword that makes this declaration a function declaration is the equal sign `=`.

The function body is—most of the time—an expression, like the call of a function or a program flow-control construct like `let-in` or `case`. Functions that return a constant value can be used to define constants at compile time (Listing 3-21).

Listing 3-21. Constant Function

```
alwaysReturn42 =
    42
```

How does the compiler know if a function we call exists? The short answer is that we have to *import* a module. This only works if we have installed the package with the needed module in our project.

Once we import a module we can use all functions that are exported (*exposed*) from the imported module. We will discuss the modularity of Elm later, so let this be a quick explanation.

Anonymous Functions

Anonymous functions are defined inline without a name. In other languages they may be called *lambda* or *delegate*.

The most important use case for anonymous functions is to pass them as arguments to other functions or to get them returned as a result of a function call.

The following example defines the function getPizzaOrders, which takes one argument of type Pizza and a second argument of type function. This function takes a Pizza as argument and returns a number (Listing 3-22).

Listing 3-22. Anonymous Functions

```
-- allbasics.elm
getPizzaOrders : Pizza -> (Pizza -> number) -> ( Pizza, number )
getPizzaOrders p calcfunction =
    let
        n = calcfunction p
    in
        (p,n)

-- elm-repl
> getPizzaOrders Calzone (\p -> if p == Calzone then 5 else 0)
(Calzone,5) : ( AllBasics.Pizza, number )
```

We can call getPizzaOrders with an anonymous function as the second argument. The definition of such a function starts with a backlash and defines the argument, and the -> tells the compiler that the following expression is the body of the function. In our case, this is a simple if construction.

An anonymous function can take more than one argument. We will see examples later in the book.

Function Composition

Normally, functions in Elm are called with the name followed by the arguments, without parentheses or commas to separate the arguments. Sometimes it is necessary to chain together function calls, where the argument of one function is the return value of another function.

The initial thought is to write the calls down as they appear. The example gets the Pizza type from a string and then calls the function pizzaLeft to determine how many pizzas are left for ordering. See Listing 3-23.

Listing 3-23. Functions for Composition

```
type Pizza = Calzone | Margherita | QuattroStagione

getPizzaFromString : String -> Maybe Pizza
getPizzaFromString p =
  case p of
    "Calzone"
      -> Just Calzone
    "Margherita"
      -> Just Margherita
    "Quattro Stagione"
      -> Just QuattroStagione

    _
      -> Nothing

pizzaLeft : Maybe Pizza -> number
pizzaLeft p =
  case p of
    Just Calzone
      -> 10

    _
      -> 0
```

When we call the functions with pizzaLeft getPizzaFromString "Calzone" we get an error because the compiler gets confused with the number of arguments. See Listing 3-24.

Listing 3-24. Composing Functions—Error

```
> pizzaLeft getPizzaFromString "Calzone"
-- TYPE MISMATCH ----------------------------------------- repl-temp-000.elm
The 1st argument to function `pizzaLeft` is causing a mismatch.
4|   pizzaLeft getPizzaFromString "Calzone"
               ^^^^^^^^^^^^^^^^^^^
Function `pizzaLeft` is expecting the 1st argument to be:
    Maybe Pizza
But it is:
    String -> Maybe Pizza
Hint: It looks like a function needs 1 more argument.
-- TYPE MISMATCH ----------------------------------------- repl-temp-000.elm
Function `pizzaLeft` is expecting 1 argument, but was given 2.
4|   pizzaLeft getPizzaFromString "Calzone"
Maybe you forgot some parentheses? Or a comma?
```

One way to fix this is to use parentheses (Listing 3-25).

Listing 3-25. Piping Functions with Parentheses

```
> pizzaLeft (getPizzaFromString "Calzone")
  10 : number
```

This compiles now, but we have a much better solution baked into the language: *function pipe operators*. We already mentioned them in the discussion about operators. When we use these operators we don't need parentheses and still get the expected result. See Listing 3-26.

Listing 3-26. Piping Functions with Operator

```
> pizzaLeft <| getPizzaFromString "Calzone"
  10 : number
> getPizzaFromString "Calzone" |> pizzaLeft
  10 : number
```

This code looks much cleaner and also expresses the intent. The left-to-right operator is a little clearer, but it is a matter of context and preferences as to which one should be used.

Polymorphic Functions

So far we have seen examples of functions that have a specified type as parameter. Sometimes, however, we want to have more generic functions. See Listing 3-27.

Listing 3-27. Polymorphic Function

```
firstListItem : List a -> Maybe a
firstListItem l =
  List.head l
```

The type annotation says that we expect a list of any type and return the first item of the list. If there is no first item it will return the value Nothing to indicate no valid result. We can run this function with any type. See Listing 3-28.

Listing 3-28. Calling a Polymorphic Function

```
import AllBasics exposing (..)
> firstListItem [1,2,3]
  Just 1 : Maybe.Maybe number
> firstListItem ["1","2","3"]
  Just "1" : Maybe.Maybe String
> firstListItem []
  Nothing : Maybe.Maybe a
```

In elm-repl we get the values with their types indicated. As promised, Maybe is a type we will discuss soon. It says, we are not sure about a value; in our case, we are not sure about the return value. This is why passing an empty list as an argument returns a value of Nothing—there is no item in the list and therefore no first item.

We said we can pass in any type as a list item, so we use a custom type we have defined (Listing 3-29).

Listing 3-29. Calling a Generic Function with a Custom Type

```
-- in AllBasics:
type alias ComposedType =
  {
    x: Int,
    y: Int,
```

```
      keypressed: Bool
  }
> import AllBasics exposing (..)
> ct = ComposedType 1 1 True
  { x = 1, y = 1, keypressed = True } : AllBasics.ComposedType
> firstListItem [ct,ct]
  Just { x = 1, y = 1, keypressed = True }
    : Maybe.Maybe AllBasics.ComposedType
```

We pass a list with custom type values as arguments and get the first item returned, as expected. We will come back to type definitions and type annotations a little bit later in this chapter.

The polymorphic function in our example made use of the module List, which handles generic values. The next example (Listing 3-30) defines a function that takes a Maybe of any type and converts the value to a string. The core module function toString is polymorphic itself.

Listing 3-30. Calling a Generic Function with a Custom Type

```
anyToString : Maybe a -> String
anyToString arg =
  case arg of
    Just arg -> toString arg
    Nothing -> "no value"
```

In the case expression we have either a valid value—the Just part—or a Nothing value. In that case, we print out a message. Running this function in elm-repl results in the output seen in Listing 3-31.

Listing 3-31. Calling a Generic Function with a Custom Type

```
> import AllBasics exposing (..)
> anyToString (Just (42))
  "42" : String
> anyToString <| Just (42)
  "42" : String
> anyToString <| Just 42
  "42" : String
```

```
> anyToString <| Just "42"
  "\"42\"" : String
> anyToString Nothing
  "no value" : String
```

The first call to `anyToString` uses parentheses. Without this the compiler would complain that we are passing two arguments to the function. Since `Just` is a constructor and thus a function, we can use the function pipe operator as described in the earlier section about operators.

Higher Order Functions

A *higher order function* is a function that takes other functions as arguments or returns a function. The concept derives from lambda calculus in mathematics, but it can be used without understanding the underlying theory. See Listing 3-32.

Listing 3-32. Higher Order Function—Lambda

```
callFunction : (a -> b) -> a -> b
callFunction func arg =
  func arg

callWithFunc : number
callWithFunc =
  callFunction (\n -> n*n) 5

callWithValue : number
callWithValue =
  let
    f = \n -> n*n
  in
    callFunction f 5
```

The example defines `callFunction`, which takes a function and an argument of any type. Its body just calls the function with the argument.

We can call this function with an anonymous function either directly or by assigning it to a variable and sending the variable to `callFunction`.

When we composed functions earlier, we used an anonymous function to calculate the pizza orders, but we can use a named function as well. See Listing 3-33.

Listing 3-33. Higher Order Function—Named Function

```
-- allbasics.elm
getPizzaOrders : Pizza -> (Pizza -> number) -> ( Pizza, number )
getPizzaOrders p calcfunction =
    let
      n = calcfunction p
    in
      (p,n)
calculatePizzaOrders : Pizza -> number
calculatePizzaOrders p =
  if  p == Calzone then
    5
  else
    0

-- elm-repl
> getPizzaOrders Margherita calculatePizzaOrders
(Margherita,0) : ( AllBasics.Pizza, number )
```

We just pass the function getPizzaOrders as an argument and get the expected result. Of course, as with the anonymous function, the named function must adhere to the function signature required.

Curried and Partial Functions

Currying is a technique that was made popular by the mathematician Haskell Curry in the 1960s. The essence is to create functions with arity 1 (that means one argument) from functions with arity greater than 1 (that means multiple arguments).

The language Haskell not surprisingly supports currying automatically, so all functions have only one argument.

The example in Listing 3-34 shows the function multiplyNumbers with two arguments and the function doubler that calls multiplyNumbers with a constant multiplier and takes one argument as its value.

Listing 3-34. Currying

```
multiplyNumbers : number -> number -> number
multiplyNumbers multiplicator value =
  multiplicator * value

doubler : number -> number
doubler =
  multiplyNumbers 2
```

When we run these two functions we see that the function doubler is just a shortcut with a constant argument (Listing 3-35).

Listing 3-35. Call Curried Function

```
> multiplyNumbers 2 21
  42 : number
> doubler 21
  42 : number
```

This is what happens (Figure 3-3):

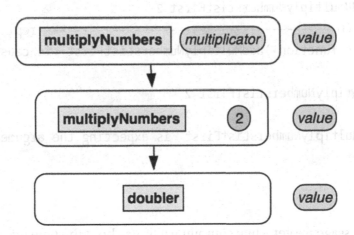

Figure 3-3. *Currying*

It is important to know that internally the same process is done when we just run multiplyNumbers 2 21. First, the function with the first argument will be defined as an internal function, and then that function will be run with the second argument. The result is exactly the same, and this process is completely transparent to the consumer of the function.

63

Functions in Elm are left-to-right associative, and they are processed in such a way that eventually every function evaluated takes one argument and returns one result.

When we manually create a curried function we need to be careful to get the argument types right. The function addMultiplyNumbersListFirst (Listing 3-36) takes a list of numbers as the first argument and a multiplier that works on the sum of all numbers in the list as the second. The function doubler should curry that function and hold the multiplier constant.

Listing 3-36. Currying Argument Position

```
-- allbasics.Elm
addNumbers : List number -> number
addNumbers list =
  List.foldr (+) 0 list

addMultiplyNumbersListFirst : List number -> number -> number
addMultiplyNumbersListFirst list m =
  addNumbers list * m

-- elm-repl
> doubler = addMultiplyNumbersListFirst 2
-- TYPE MISMATCH --------------------------------------- repl-temp-000.elm
The argument to function `addMultiplyNumbersListFirst` is causing a
mismatch.
5|        addMultiplyNumbersListFirst 2
                                      ^
Function `addMultiplyNumbersListFirst` is expecting the argument to be:
    List number
But it is:
    number
```

The error message we get while compiling tells us about the type mismatch. The number 2 is interpreted as a list, but it is of type number. The solution to this problem is to flip the arguments, and luckily there is a function in the standard library that does exactly that: flip. See Listing 3-37.

Listing 3-37. Flip

```
> addMultiplyNumbersListFirst
  <function> : List number -> number -> number
> flip addMultiplyNumbersListFirst
  <function> : number -> List number -> number
> doubler = flip addMultiplyNumbersListFirst 2
  <function> : List number -> number
> doubler [1,2,3]
  12 : number
```

The function `flip` changes the order of the arguments, which allows us to define `doubler` as before. The original function `addMultiplyNumbersListFirst` is not changed, of course. With `flip` we created a new unnamed function and combined it with the number 2 to become a new function.

What happens if we have more than two arguments? The function `multiplyAndConcatenate` has three arguments in the next example (Listing 3-38). It adds the numbers of the list and multiplies the result by the multiplier. Then, it converts the resulting number to a string and concatenates it with another string.

Listing 3-38. Flip with Three Arguments

```
addNumbers : List number -> number
addNumbers list =
  List.foldr (+) 0 list

multiplyAndConcatenate : List number -> number -> String -> String
multiplyAndConcatenate list multi s =
  toString (addNumbers list * multi) ++ s

> multiplyAndConcatenate [1,2,3] 2 ""
  "12" : String
> f = flip multiplyAndConcatenate
  <function> : number -> List number -> String -> String
> doubler = f 2
  <function> : List number -> String -> String
```

```
> doubler [1,2,3] ""
  "12" : String
> doubler [1,2,3] "List values doubled"
  "12 List values doubled" : String
```

When we flip the arguments, only the first two arguments are flipped. This helps us to define another function `doubler`. First, we define the function `f`, which takes the same three arguments, but with the first two in reverse order. Then, we create a partial function from `f` and keep the multiplier constant as 2. With that done, we can now call our `doubler` function `d` with two arguments: the list of numbers and the string. As a side note, do not use function names like `f` or `d` in production code—the next developer reading your code will be grateful.

This example looks very much constructed, and honestly it is. I was looking through my code and could not find many examples with three arguments. The few I found did not have different argument types, so were not right to show flipping arguments. When I write functions I keep them very simple, and if more than two arguments are used it is better to wrap them in a structured type.

Note *Curried functions* and *partial functions* are not the same, but they are related. *Currying* means to create functions with one argument and return one result. Partial functions have more than one argument and return one result. So, we can argue that a curried function is a partial function, but not vice versa.

We can mix currying and composition to define functions as well. We have already used some of the functions in the following example. The function `multiplyNumbers` just takes two numbers and returns the product, and `doubler` holds the multiplier constant at 2.

We want to add all the numbers in a list and pass it to `doubler`. Instead of creating a new function, we compose existing ones (Listing 3-39).

Listing 3-39. Currying with Composition

```
-- allbasics.elm
addNumbers : List number -> number
addNumbers list =
  List.foldr (+) 0 list
```

```
multiplyNumbers : number -> number -> number
multiplyNumbers multiplicator value =
  value * multiplicator

doubler : number -> number
doubler =
  multiplyNumbers 2

-- elm-repl
> adddoubleleft = addNumbers >> doubler
  <function:_user$project$Repl$adddoubleleft> : List number -> number
> adddoubleleft [1,2,3]
  12 : number
> adddoubleright = doubler << addNumbers
  <function:_user$project$Repl$adddoubleright> : List number -> number
> adddoubleright [1,2,3]
  12 : number
```

The functions adddoubleleft and adddoubleright only differ in their use of the composition operator; the result is the same. We compose a function with addNumbers and doubler to create a function that takes a list of numbers and returns the result as a number. Neither multiplyNumbers nor the derived function doubler know anything about lists; their arguments are just piped in from a different function. The consumer of the adddouble functions is not aware of the composition at all.

Immutable Data

All values in Elm are immutable. After a value is defined it cannot be changed, and there is no way around it. The example function immutableTest tries to redefine the symbol a. The compiler does not agree with it as we expect (Listing 3-40).

Listing 3-40. Immutable Data

```
-- allbasics.elm
immutableTest =
  let
    a = 120
    a = addNumbers [1,2,3]
```

```
  in
    a
```

```
-- elm-repl
-- DUPLICATE DEFINITION ------------------------------------ allbasics.elm
There are multiple values named `a` in this let-expression.
98|     a = addNumbers [1,2,3]
        ^
```

Search through this let-expression, find all the values named `a`, and give each of them a unique name.

Caution   Unfortunately, `elm-repl` lets you redefine symbols. Typing in a = 120 will define a with the constant 120. If you type then a = `addNumbers [1,2,3]` then a will have the result of the function call.

Data structures are immutable as well. For example, when we change a value in a list a new list will be created and returned. The original list will not be altered. All this contributes to side effect–free applications. When an argument is passed, there is no way that the value of the argument will have been changed.

State

The Elm platform is created for web applications. HTTP, the underlying protocol, is stateless, and so should be the web applications. On the other side, the rise of client-only applications in browsers causes a demand for state.

Elm—as a functional language with immutable data—does not support global state, but similar to actor models, which pass messages, a state can be wrapped in message models.

The model passed around in an Elm application has to cater to the state of modules and also for a global state that is not attached to just one module. The following example (Listing 3-41) shows two types that define various values.

Listing 3-41. State

```
type alias Event =
  { timestamp: Int
  , eventname: String
  }
type alias Model  =
  { xpos : Int
  , ypos : Int
  , numbertones: Int
  , backgroundimage: String
  , events: List Event
  }
```

The type Event is a global state that is passed into the type Model. Every module that has an event to add to the list can do this. In a real situation we want to minimize the message footprint, so most likely we would persist the event list on a regular basis.

We will examine the Elm architecture and how it supports models and messages in Chapter 5.

Recursion

In the section about control structures we mentioned that functional programming uses recursive functions instead of loops.

The following code (Listing 3-42) shows a function that returns a string that is a substitution for a token found with a regex expression. The argument poslist is a list of those tokens. The function replaceText is similar, as it just replaces string in a string passed as an argument and returns a new string. Other functions that are called from this function are not shown. See Listing 3-42.

Listing 3-42. Recursion

```
replace : List String -> String -> String
replace poslist markdown =
  case poslist of
  [] -> (markdown)
```

```
first :: rest ->
  let
    newmd = replaceText first (getsubstitution first) markdown
  in
    replace rest newmd
```

Iterating through a list always follows the same pattern. If the list is not empty, we get the first element (`first`), process it, and then call the same function recursively with the rest of the list (`rest`).

In our example, processing the element in `poslist` means to get a new string. We process this string `markdown` by passing it to another function, `replaceText`, and use the returned value. The rest of our initial input list calls the `return` function recursively until the list is empty. When the list is empty, the string with the replacements is returned as the result of the function.

Many JavaScript engines do not implement tail-call elimination, but the Elm compiler optimizes tail-recursive calls as much as possible. For certain deep recursions the stack can still grow too large and cause runtime problems. The Elm platform provides the module `Trampoline` that helps in this situation.

Pattern Matching and Deconstructing

Pattern matching in its simplest form means to check data for an exact pattern. It is common in functional programming and shows its full power when the data checked is the *AST* (Abstract Syntax Tree). Then, languages like Elixir can extend the language with macros that manipulate the AST or allow overloaded functions.

Deconstructing is related to pattern matching, but it is restricted to certain types. Values are extracted from the type and bound to symbols like a variable.

Values

The example in Listing 3-43 is a simplified version of the recursive function we looked at before. The `case` construct uses pattern matching to determine which expression to evaluate. In our code, the argument `markdown` is returned when the list `poslist` is empty. In all other cases, it returns an empty string. The underscore can always be used when we are not interested in a pattern-matched value.

Listing 3-43. Pattern Matching—Values

```
replace : List String -> String -> String
replace poslist markdown =
  case poslist of
    [] ->
      (markdown)
    _ ->
      ""
```

Tuples

The function getPizzaTupleAsString receives a tuple with elements of type Pizza and returns a string. To get the string presentations of the tuple elements, we first need to get the elements as values. The expression (pz1, pz2) = t takes the tuple and matches each element to the local symbols pz1 and pz2. These can then be used to get the string with the standard library function toString. See Listing 3-44.

Listing 3-44. Pattern Matching—Tuples

```
type Pizza = Calzone | Margherita | QuattroStagione

getPizzaTupleAsString : (Pizza, Pizza) -> String
getPizzaTupleAsString t =
  let
    (pz1, pz2) = t
  in
    toString pz1 ++ "," ++ toString pz2
```

Lists

Lists work in a way similar to tuples, but with a different syntax—the ( ) is replaced by [ ]. There is a big difference, though. The implementation in Listing 3-45 causes a compile error.

Listing 3-45. Pattern Matching—Lists

```
getPizzaListAsString : List Pizza -> String
getPizzaListAsString l =
  let
    [pz1, pz2] = l
  in
    toString pz1 ++ "," ++ toString pz2

{-- PARTIAL PATTERN -------------------------------------- allbasics.elm
The pattern used here does not cover all possible values.
244|      [pz1, pz2] = l
You need to account for the following values:
    []
    _ :: []
    _ :: _ :: _ :: _
Switch to a `case` expression to handle all possible patterns.
-}
```

Tuples can't be empty, but lists can be, and they can have one element or many. The compiler forces us to implement code for all these possibilities and also tells us to use a case construct. See Listing 3-46.

Listing 3-46. Pattern Matching—Tuples

```
type Pizza = Calzone | Margherita | QuattroStagione

getPizzaListAsString : List Pizza -> String
getPizzaListAsString l =
  case l of
    [pz1,pz2] ->
      toString pz1 ++ "," ++ toString pz2
    [pz1] ->
      toString pz1
    pz1 :: pz2 :: _ ->
      toString pz1 ++ "," ++ toString pz2 ++ " ... and more"
    [] ->
      "List empty"
```

The code compiles, but has one problem, which is directly related to Elm's desire to not cause runtime errors. If the list we pass as an argument has more than two or three elements, we have to implement all these cases to get the concatenated string we want as a result. The wildcard, as indicated in the compiler error text in Listing 3-45, would not work, because we don't want to ignore the values.

If we think about the problem, we see that our implementation algorithm is not correct. We have to use a recursive function—either a custom implementation or, better yet, a standard library function like foldl (see Chapter 4).

Records

We have seen records before when encountering types. They define key–value pairs where values don't need to be of only one type. In our example, all values are of type Pizza, though. Pattern matching records works like it does with tuples. We only need to ensure that the symbols we use for the pattern-matched values have exactly the same names as the ones we defined in the record. See Listing 3-47.

Listing 3-47. Pattern Matching—Records

```
type Pizza = Calzone | Margherita | QuattroStagione

getPizzaRecordAsString : { a | pz1 : Pizza, pz2 : Pizza } -> String
getPizzaRecordAsString r =
  let
    {pz1, pz2} = r
  in
    toString pz1 ++ ", " ++ toString pz2
```

If we call with a record that has an invalid key we get an error message (Listing 3-48).

Listing 3-48. Pattern Matching—Records Error

```
> getPizzaRecordAsString {pz1 = Calzone, pz2= Margherita }
  "Calzone, Margherita" : String
> getPizzaRecordAsString {pz1 = Calzone, p= Margherita }
-- TYPE MISMATCH ------------------------------------- repl-temp-000.elm
The argument to function `getPizzaRecordAsString` is causing a mismatch.
7|    getPizzaRecordAsString {pz1 = Calzone, p= Margherita }
                 ^^^^^^^^^^^^^^^^^^^^^^^^^^^^^^^^^^^^^^
```

73

```
Function `getPizzaRecordAsString` is expecting the argument to be:
    { a | ..., pz2 : ... }
But it is:
    { ..., p : ... }
Hint: The record fields do not match up. Maybe you made one of these typos?
    pz2 <-> pz1
```

Types

We can pattern match union types as well. The example in Listing 3-49 defines a type
with an integer as additional information. We will examine types in Elm in the next
section.

In the case construct we get this additional value and thus can work with it. Again,
the value is a local value, while the original value is immutable.

Listing 3-49. Pattern Matching—Types

```
-- allbasics.elm
type Pizza
  = Calzone Int
  | Margherita Int
  | QuattroStagione Int

getPizzaOrders : Pizza -> Int
getPizzaOrders p =
    case p of
      Calzone n -> n
      Margherita n -> n
      QuattroStagione n -> n

-- elm-repl
> p = Calzone 5
Calzone 5 : AllBasics.Pizza
> getPizzaOrders p
5 : Int
```

Elm as a Type-safe Language

Programming languages can be roughly divided in two groups: the first one has *dynamic typing* and the second has *static typing*. There are more divisions within these groups, but they are not relevant for our discussion.

Dynamic typing means that variables can hold values of any type, and its interpretation depends on the context. Examples of dynamically typed languages include Ruby, JavaScript, and Elixir. Some dynamically typed languages may check the types at runtime or alternatively during code analysis before deployment, but normally incorrect interpretations will be detected at runtime and may cause exceptions if problems were not detected during tests.

Users of Elm say that they have not experienced runtime errors. This has to do with type checks during the compilation of Elm code. Types are inferred during compilation or by interpreting type annotations. Elm is a statically typed language.

Types

Elm has types that are similar to those from other languages, but also types that need a bit more explanation and are either connected to ideas of functional languages or the Elm platform itself.

Primitives

The type number can be either Float or Int. Conversions are performed automatically depending on the operator. For example, the division of two integers with / returns a float. See Listing 3-50.

Listing 3-50. Numbers

```
> 1
  1 : number
> 1.0
  1 : Float
> 5 / 2
  2.5 : Float
> 5 // 2
  2 : Int
```

Strings are defined with a double quote " and characters with a single quote '. They cannot be concatenated without conversion functions, which we will see when we discuss basic standard libraries in Chapter 4. See Listing 3-51.

Listing 3-51. Strings and Chars

```
> "Hello"
"Hello" : String
> 'H'
'H' : Char
```

Comparable Types

Comparison operators like >= or < work with *comparable* types. These are defined as numbers, characters, strings, and lists, as well as tuples of those. On both sides of the comparison, the comparable types must be the same. See Listing 3-52.

Listing 3-52. Comparable Types

```
> 1 > 2.0
  False : Bool
> 1.0 < 2.0
  True : Bool
> 'a' < 'z'
  True : Bool
> "a" < "z"
  True : Bool
> "Hello" > "World"
  False : Bool
> (1,2) > (0,3)
  True : Bool
> ['1','2'] < ['3','1']
  True : Bool
```

Appendable Types

The ++ operator works with *appendable* types. These are defined as strings and lists of any type that is allowed to be an element of a list. See Listing 3-53.

Listing 3-53. Appendable Types

```
> "a" ++ "b"
  "ab" : String
> [1,2] ++ [1,2]
  [1,2,1,2] : List number
```

Structured Data

The basic structured data types in Elm are List, Tuple, and Record. List has several derived data types like Dict Array and Set, which are defined in the standard library (see Chapter 4).

Lists

Lists define values of the same type. Mixing the value types will throw a compile error. See Listing 3-54.

Listing 3-54. List

```
> ["Calzone", "Margherita", "QuattroStagione"]
  ["Calzone","Margherita","QuattroStagione"] : List String
> []
  [] : List a
> "Calzone" :: ["Margherita", "QuattroStagione"]
  ["Calzone","Margherita","QuattroStagione"] : List String
> [1, "a"] -- ERROR
-- TYPE MISMATCH ------------------------------------- repl-temp-000.elm
The 1st and 2nd entries in this list are different types of values.
5|    [1, "a"]
```

Tuples

Tuples are defined in a similar way to lists, but they have a constructor. The second definition in Listing 3-55 tells the compiler to construct a tuple with three elements and passes the values as arguments to the constructor function. Tuples do not need to have the same value types.

Listing 3-55. Tuple

```
> ("Calzone", Calzone, 5)
  ("Calzone",Calzone,5) : ( String, Pizza, number )
> (,,) "Calzone" Calzone 5
  ("Calzone",Calzone,5) : ( String, Pizza, number )
```

Records

Records have key–value pairs as elements without the restriction that elements need to have the same type. Key names must start with a lowercase character and must be unique within a record.

Values can be accessed with a dot notation. Key names not in the record which are tried to be accessed with the dot will throw a compiler error.

Updating a record value returns a new record. The original record is not changed. See Listing 3-56.

Listing 3-56. Record

```
> p = {name = "Calzone",order = 5, pizza = Calzone}
  { name = "Calzone", order = 5, pizza = Calzone }
    : { name : String, order : number, pizza : AllBasics.Pizza }
> p.name
  "Calzone" : String
> p.order
  5 : number
> p.pizza
  Calzone : AllBasics.Pizza
> pupdated = { p | order = 8 }
    { name = "Calzone", order = 8, pizza = Calzone }
      : { name : String, pizza : AllBasics.Pizza, order : number }
> p.order
  5 : number
> pupdated.order
  8 : number
```

Type Definitions

In the preceding sections we discussed built-in types. Elm lets us define custom types as well, although in a different way than in other mainly imperative languages. In addition, the language knows types that add features to custom types.

Union Types

The name *union type* comes from the fact that several types are defined in one larger type. Elm calls the defined types *tags*, and the union type as such is a *tagged union*. Each tag is like a constructor and can have parameters. All names start with an uppercase character.

We saw the following example when we discussed pattern matching and did not explain the "additional information." As it is a constructor, it makes sense that the tag can have arguments passed into it. The name of the type—`Pizza`—is only used in type annotations (see later). We construct a new instance of a `Pizza` type by calling the `tag` function with an argument that can be a constant, a constant from a variable, or an expression. See Listing 3-57.

Listing 3-57. Union Type

```
-- allbasics.elm
type Pizza
  = Calzone Int
  | Margherita Int
  | QuattroStagione Int

-- elm-repl
> Calzone 5
  Calzone 5 : AllBasics.Pizza
> n = 12
  12 : number
> Calzone n
  Calzone 12 : AllBasics.Pizza
> Calzone (n*3)
  Calzone 36 : AllBasics.Pizza
```

Type Aliases

We could define our data model with basic types and pass the values as arguments to functions. When we discussed partial functions and currying we saw the importance of having fewer parameters. With *type aliases* we can create more complex types, which also helps to make type annotations easier to read.

Basically, a type alias is a record with key–value pairs, as we have seen before, and the type name always starts with an uppercase character. Models in the Elm architecture are defined with this type. See Listing 3-58.

Listing 3-58. Type Alias

```
type alias Event =
  { timestamp: Int
  , eventname: String
  }

type alias Model  =
  { xpos : Int
  , ypos : Int
  , numbertones: Int
  , backgroundimage: String
  , events: List Event
  }
```

Maybe

In JavaScript and other languages, a null value may be returned by functions, often causing runtime errors. In Elm we have Maybe, which can represent values that exist or do not exist. The type Maybe is a union type itself, with the members Just a and Nothing. The latter is the equivalent of null in other languages. Just means that there is a valid value, and it is the argument to the Just constructor that returns a Maybe.

Remember the pattern-matching examples? When we pattern match a union type with a parameter we get the argument in a pattern-matched clause. This is what the example function anyToString uses. If there is a valid value it returns the value converted to a string; otherwise, it returns a string with a message. See Listing 3-59.

Listing 3-59. Maybe

```
anyToString : Maybe a -> String
anyToString arg =
  case arg of
    Just arg -> toString arg
    Nothing -> "no value"
```

This is just a quick look at Maybe. We will discuss it more in Chapter 4.

Constants

There is no type Constant in Elm, but we can define one with a constant function. Whenever we need the constant value we can call the function. See Listing 3-60.

Listing 3-60. Constant

```
returnOnly42 =
  42
```

Type Annotations

Type annotations in Elm are optional, but it is not recommended that you leave them out. Compiling code with the elm-make option --warn will print out missing annotations that can then be copied into the code file.

How can we read type annotations? It always starts with the name of the function and a colon :, which means "has type." If there are no arguments, a type name will follow next and end the type annotation. If there are arguments, the type names are listed followed by an arrow ->. Types like functions, tuples, or records have a special syntax. It is not too difficult to read those, so soon you will be able to read the type annotations without problems. See Listing 3-61.

Listing 3-61. Type Annotation

```
varassign_to_tuple : ( String, number )
addMultiplyNumbers : number -> List number -> number
addPizza : List Pizza -> Pizza -> List Pizza
getPizzaRecordAsString : { a | pz1 : Pizza, pz2 : Pizza } -> String
```

We have already seen most of the examples, so they will look familiar. The function *varassign_to_tuple* takes no argument and returns a tuple.

Unit Type

We saw that we can define polymorphic functions by providing not a type name, but rather a type variable. The following example (Listing 3-62) shows that we can do the same with types. We define EventDescription with the type of attachment unspecified.

We can now create this type with different types for attachment; for example, as a list of strings. The function getEventAttachment specifies this in the type annotation and works with the defined record.

If we don't want to use attachment, we can assign the unit type () to it. This indicates that there is no value available. To use this record we can define the same in the function type annotation. This is one example where the type annotation should be written because the compiler will not infer what we want to do.

Listing 3-62. Unit Type

```
-- allbasics.elm
type alias EventDescription a =
  { title : String
  , text : String
  , attachment : a
  }

getEventAttachment : EventDescription (List String) -> List String
getEventAttachment ev =
  ev.attachment

getEventDescriptionUnitType : EventDescription () -> String
getEventDescriptionUnitType ev =
  ev.title

-- elm-repl
> ev = {title="title",text = "text", attachment = ["a","b"]}
  { title = "title", text = "text", attachment = ["a","b"] }
    : { attachment : List String, text : String, title : String }
```

```
> getEventAttachment ev
  ["a","b"] : List String
> ev2 = {title="title",text = "text", attachment = ()}
{ title = "title", text = "text", attachment = () }
    : { attachment : (), text : String, title : String }
> getEventDescriptionUnitType ev2
"title" : String
```

Elm as a Modular Language

Elm uses modules to separate functions and create a namespace. These modules can be compiled as packages and then published. A package is a module like any other, but has different documentation requirements.

Modules

A module is defined with the keyword module, with the name following, along with the exposing keyword with a list of all functions that should be exported from the module. If we don't want to list the functions, we can use (..) to export everything. See Listing 3-63.

Listing 3-63. Module

```
module AllBasics exposing (..)

module AllBasics exposing (addNumbers, addMultiplyNumbers)
```

Imports

In several examples we have imported modules. The keyword import tells the compiler which module we need. The module name is followed by the keyword exposing, with the list of functions, as in the module declaration. We can import everything with (..), but it makes sense to indicate exactly which functions to use, otherwise all the compiled code of the module will have to be copied to the JavaScript file.

Importing requires choosing one of the following three options:

- With `exposing`: We can use unqualified functions; e.g., `addNumbers`.

- Without `exposing`: We have to use qualified names; e.g., `AllBasics.addNumbers`.

- With alias, like import `AllBasics` as `AB`. Then, we use the qualified name `AB.addNumbers`. See Listing 3-64.

Listing 3-64. Module Imports

```
import AllBasics exposing (..)

import AllBasics exposing (addNumbers)
import Html exposing (text)

import AllBasics
import AllBasics as AB
```

What We Learned

This chapter had a lot of information in it, as follows:

- We saw what the Elm platform offers us.

- We looked at code adhering to the Elm style guide.

- We learned the basics of the Elm language from different points of view: functional, typed, and modular.

In the next chapter, we will examine the tools available on the Elm platform and have a look at some of the basic standard libraries.

CHAPTER 4

Tooling and Libraries

In the previous two chapters, we set up our development environment and learned the basics of the Elm language. Now, we want to explore the tooling the Elm platform provides and get an overview of standard libraries.

This chapter will cover the following topics:

- How to test small code snippets with the REPL
- Ways to get a head start on a project with scaffolding
- How we can build our project
- An overview of standard libraries that come with the Elm platform

REPL

It seems that any platform needs to have an REPL (*read-eval-print-loop*) nowadays, or it is not taken seriously. It is certainly a matter of preference whether a developer uses an REPL or not. This tool is very useful for exploring the language and standard or third-party libraries.

We already used the Elm REPL to learn aspects of the language in the previous two chapters. Now, we want to explore more options and use cases.

We can start elm-repl with the elm command (Listing 4-1).

Listing 4-1. elm-repl

```
$ elm repl
---- elm-repl 0.18.0 -------------------------------------------------------
 :help for help, :exit to exit, more at <https://github.com/elm-lang/elm-repl>
----------------------------------------------------------------------------
> _
```

© Wolfgang Loder 2018
W. Loder, *Web Applications with Elm*, https://doi.org/10.1007/978-1-4842-2610-0_4

As with other Elm command-line commands, a program is called in the background. In this case it is `elm-repl`. We could run this executable directly and would get the same results.

We see a banner with version information and a hint about two commands we can use from within `elm-repl` to get help or exit. The prompt in the last line indicates that the REPL is ready to receive commands. If we type in the command `:help`, we see what's shown in Listing 4-2.

Listing 4-2.

```
> :help
General usage directions: <https://github.com/elm-lang/elm-repl#elm-repl>
Additional commands available from the prompt:

  :help              List available commands
  :flags             Manipulate flags sent to elm compiler
  :reset             Clears all previous imports
  :exit              Exits elm-repl
```

The command `:flags` can be used to manipulate compiler flags in the REPL. In version 0.18 there is only one flag allowed (`--src-dir`). This defines a directory that can be used for source code we use in the REPL; otherwise, it just uses the project directory we are starting `elm-repl` from and uses the `elm-project.json` file located there.

So, what can we do with `elm-repl`? We can use expressions with the operators discussed in Chapter 3, we can define functions and types, and we can import modules.

The expressions in Listing 4-3 look familiar from Chapter 3, where we used similar expressions learning the language.

Listing 4-3.

```
> s1 = "hello world"
  "hello world" : String
> l1 = List.range 1 4
  [1,2,3,4] : List Int
> s2 = s1 ++ " " ++ toString pi
  "hello world 3.141592653589793" : String
> 42 + pi - 1
  44.1415926535898 : Float
```

All the preceding examples can be typed into elm-repl without importing additional modules. Some functions and modules are part of elm-core and are automatically imported and immediately available; see later in this chapter which modules and functions are available from the start. We can also define functions and types in elm-repl (Listings 4-4 and 4-5).

Listing 4-4.

```
> multiplyNumbers value multiplicator = value * multiplicator
  <function> : number -> number -> number
> returnOnly42 = 42
  42 : number
> multiplyNumbers returnOnly42 42
  1764 : number
```

Listing 4-5.

```
> type Pizza = Calzone | Margherita
> type alias Pos = { x:Int, y:Int }
```

Usage of the REPL gets a little bit more complicated if several modules are defined as dependencies. What happens if we want to use a function that is unknown to elm-repl? In the example in Listing 4-6 we want to get the length of a string.

Listing 4-6.

```
> length "string"
-- NAMING ERROR ------------------------------------- repl-temp-000.elm
Cannot find variable `length`
3|   length "string"
     ^^^^^^
Maybe you want one of the following?
    List.length

> String.length "string"
-- NAMING ERROR ------------------------------------- repl-temp-000.elm
Cannot find variable `String.length`.
3|   String.length "string"
     ^^^^^^^^^^^^^
```

```
No module called `String` has been imported.
> import String
> String.length "string"
  6 : Int
```

The compiler does not know exactly what we want, but the hints give us the impression there may be a `String.length` available, although `List.length` is suggested. Eventually, we get the correct hint to import a module. We do so, and the expression is finally working.

Note   As we will see later, `string` is implemented as a list; therefore, we get `List.Length` as the first suggestion.

When we type an expression in `elm-repl` or import a module, the source code is implemented into a temporary module. We can import our own modules and change it while `elm-repl` is running. It will pick up the changes and recompile.

Not all features of the language are available in `elm-repl`. For example, it does not understand *type annotations*, and definitions of operators did not work in the Elm platform version I used for this book as well (Listing 4-7).

Listing 4-7.

```
> f : Int -> Int \
| f n = n
  -- SYNTAX PROBLEM ----------------------------------- repl-temp-000.elm

  A single colon is for type annotations. Maybe you want :: instead? Or
  maybe you
  are defining a type annotation, but there is whitespace before it?
  5| f : Int -> Int
  Maybe <http://elm-lang.org/docs/syntax> can help you figure it out.

> f n = n
  <function:_user$project$Repl$f> : a -> a
```

The compiler detects that a type annotation is intended, but can't resolve what we write. The backlash at the end of the line tells `elm-repl` that we want to type in multiple lines and that the text should only be evaluated once we press Enter without a backlash at the end of the line.

In the last line we see a type annotation returned that shows a strange name. This is the name of the module that the REPL has created. Every function must be defined in a module, and in the REPL the creation of a temporary module is done automatically. When we exit elm-repl all definitions of the session will be lost.

Defining functions in the REPL is working, and we will get a type annotation returned. Being unable to evaluate type annotations is not a problem unless we have or want to specify exactly what types we expect as arguments (Listing 4-8).

Listing 4-8.

```
> (++*) list multiplicator = 42

-- SYNTAX PROBLEM ------------------------------------- repl-temp-000.elm
I ran into something unexpected when parsing your code!
5|    ++*
       ^
I am looking for one of the following things:
    an expression
    whitespace
```

This operator definition is an abbreviated example from allbasics.elm. It seems that elm-repl does not recognize the parentheses and throws an error. This and the preceding problem may have been fixed in the version you are using.

We have just seen a multiline example. The following code (Listing 4-9) defines a function over several lines that can be called in the REPL from that point on. As mentioned before, this function definition is local to elm-repl and is lost when exiting with :exit.

Listing 4-9.

```
> varassign_to_tuple = \
|   let \
|     s1 = "hello world" \
|     s2 = 42 \
|   in \
|     (s1,s2)

  ("hello world",42) : ( String, number )
```

The REPL—as is the language—is very picky with whitespace. For example, in the preceding code the let and in need to be aligned on the same column and indented. This is not a big problem in an editor, but makes typing longer functions into elm-repl cumbersome.

Overall, Elm's REPL is sufficient for testing expressions or small functions. It is more powerful when we import our modules to test some of our functions manually. This is the approach we took in the previous chapter to learn Elm. Once we apply the Elm architecture and build web applications, the REPL is not a good way to test anymore.

In any case, elm-repl is not a replacement—nor is it meant to be—for in-depth testing. It's a tool for trying out ideas or getting to know the functions of a module that may be used in an application. It serves well up to a point in the development process.

Development Process

Developing an Elm application involves several tools from the Elm platform and beyond (Figure 4-1).

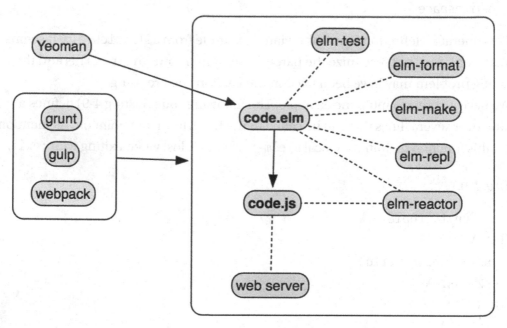

Figure 4-1. *Elm development process*

In the center of the process are the Elm code files. In the diagram, we have only one file displayed, but every non-trivial application will have more than one. We will touch on code organization in Chapter 5.

The code files are compiled with `elm-make` and manually tested in `elm-repl` and `elm-reactor`. We format the code with `elm-format` and run unit tests with `elm-test`. The output of the compilation is a JavaScript file that can be run in a web server.

On the left side of the diagram we see a list of tools that are supporting this process. What many of them—and all in the diagram—have in common is that they are Node.js tools, which emphasizes the integration of the Elm platform into that ecosystem. The next two sections have more information about those tools.

Scaffolding

When we start a project we may want to get a head start with pre-built project skeletons that support building the projects and debugging them. The Elm platform does not provide a scaffolding tool. Simple applications are not too difficult to set up, but if we want a little bit more then we have to organize our code better than simply having everything in one file or even one directory.

Searching for Elm scaffolding solutions reveals several attempts by the Elm community to bootstrap a project. Some are written in Python, some in Haskell, and many in JavaScript.

One of the most used scaffolding tools for web applications is *Yeoman*.[1] The tool itself is a framework for generators; at the moment there are more than 7,000 generators in the database. Not all are updated regularly, and many won't work with the latest versions of frameworks, but the rest add up to an impressive number.

We can find a few Elm generators, but again not all of them were updated to handle the latest version. Nevertheless, let's try one and go through the process of setting up a new project. I assume you have set up Yeoman on your computer.

Note   In Listing 4-10 we are using Yeoman in the current directory. To avoid overwriting files, create a new directory, change into it, and then run the following commands.

---

[1]`http://yeoman.io/`

91

Listing 4-10.

```
$ npm install generator-elm
$ yo elm .

<ascii art omitted>

Going to create project in folder: ~/Projects/bookcompanion-elm/Scaffolding
? Project name? Scaffolding
>
    create
    (omitted)

Starting downloads...

    ● elm-lang/virtual-dom 2.0.4
    ● elm-lang/html 2.0.0
    ● elm-lang/core 5.1.1

Packages configured successfully!

    Project generated

    1. Start dev server: npm start
    2. Visit <http://localhost:3000>
    3. Make changes to src/Main.elm
```

The installation of the generator takes a while and installs several Node packages in the Yeoman folder. Generating a new project goes through downloading about 250 MB of Node packages and then compiles the project. There is only one option for the project name in this generator.

This generator uses *webpack* to build the application. It provides all necessary scripts in package.json and also sets up the configuration file webpack.config.js. A readme file explains the steps to build and run the application. The provided code file is a simple *Hello World* example that implements all parts of the Elm architecture in one file.

Most of the time scaffolding solutions are opinionated and force the user to use certain tools. The concepts come from JavaScript development and use its tools. In this section, we created a project that uses *webpack^ for building; the next section looks at other solutions.

Building

When we develop an Elm application we want to automate as much as possible, as follows:

- Compile changed files automatically.
- Build distribution files.
- Invoke tools easily.
- Run a web server with the compiled files.
- Support JavaScript frameworks and CSS creation.

Luckily, we can use the same tools the JavaScript web community has created. Apart from Webpack[2] mentioned in the previous section, we also have Gulp[3] and Grunt[4] available.

All the previously mentioned tools require configurations and use many other Node packages to do their jobs. If you just want to watch Elm files and compile them when they have changed, a more lightweight solution would be Chokidar[5] or Chokidar-cli.[6] The following script (Listing 4-11) can be integrated into the *scripts* section in `package.json`.

Listing 4-11.

```
"watch": "chokidar '**/*.elm' -c 'elm make allbasics.elm
    --output elm.js --warn' --initial"
```

Whenever a file changes, the main file `allbasics.elm` and dependent files will be compiled with the `--warn` option. The tool has many more options and is used by other build tools, like the aforementioned Gulp or Webpack.

This is not the place to go much deeper into the configuration of the different build tools, which would almost require a small book of its own. A development team will use what they are comfortable with. Build tools working together with scaffolding and editor plugins are the key to successfully implementing Elm applications that are bigger than a simple *Hello World*.

---

[2]https://webpack.github.io/
[3]https://www.npmjs.com/package/gulp-elm
[4]https://www.npmjs.com/package/grunt-elm
[5]https://github.com/paulmillr/chokidar
[6]https://github.com/kimmobrunfeldt/chokidar-cli

Switch Elm Versions

At the moment there is no official solution for switching versions of the Elm platform. The rapid development of Elm makes it necessary to have different projects use different Elm platform versions.

There are workarounds with local and global installations as described in Chapter 2. As the name says, they are workarounds, and it would be nice to have a switch tool baked into the platform.

Debugging

The Elm platform prides itself on having no runtime errors because of the language design and application compilation. At least, this is the information we get from companies that have actually used Elm in production.

Sometimes we want to know what is going on in our application when we run it in a browser. The Elm platform development is still working on a solution to achieve the debugging of a reactive application in the browser. There were solutions before[7] that are on hold now.

One way to "look" into an application is to print information out. We've done this for decades, and the method is still used; for example, in JavaScript. Functional languages like Elm and asynchronous programs don't lend themselves easily to employing this. Therefore, we find in the Elm core libraries the module Debug, but the warning in the documentation is to not use it in production.

The first function in the following example—debuggerTestString—uses log to print out debug information on the console. From the perspective of functional programming, this is not a pure function but rather a side effect. The second function—debuggerTestCrash—crashes the application with a custom message. See Listing 4-12.

Listing 4-12.

```
import Debug exposing (..)

debuggerTestString : String -> Int
debuggerTestString s =
  length (log "s" s)
```

---

[7]http://debug.elm-lang.org/

```
debuggerTestCrash =
  crash "Not implemented"
```

When we run these functions in elm-repl, we get the output seen in Listing 4-13.

Listing 4-13.

```
> debuggerTestString "Hello"
  s: "Hello"
  5 : Int
> debuggerTestCrash
  Error: Ran into a `Debug.crash` in module `AllBasics` on line 11
  The message provided by the code author is:
      Not implemented
```

Printing out debug information is not always possible. When we run the application in the browser, we need a direct look into the state of the application. The following screenshot is from a test page of a simple game framework (Figure 4-2). The line at the top of the page displays the state whenever the values are updated. Updates are triggered when the mouse position changes.

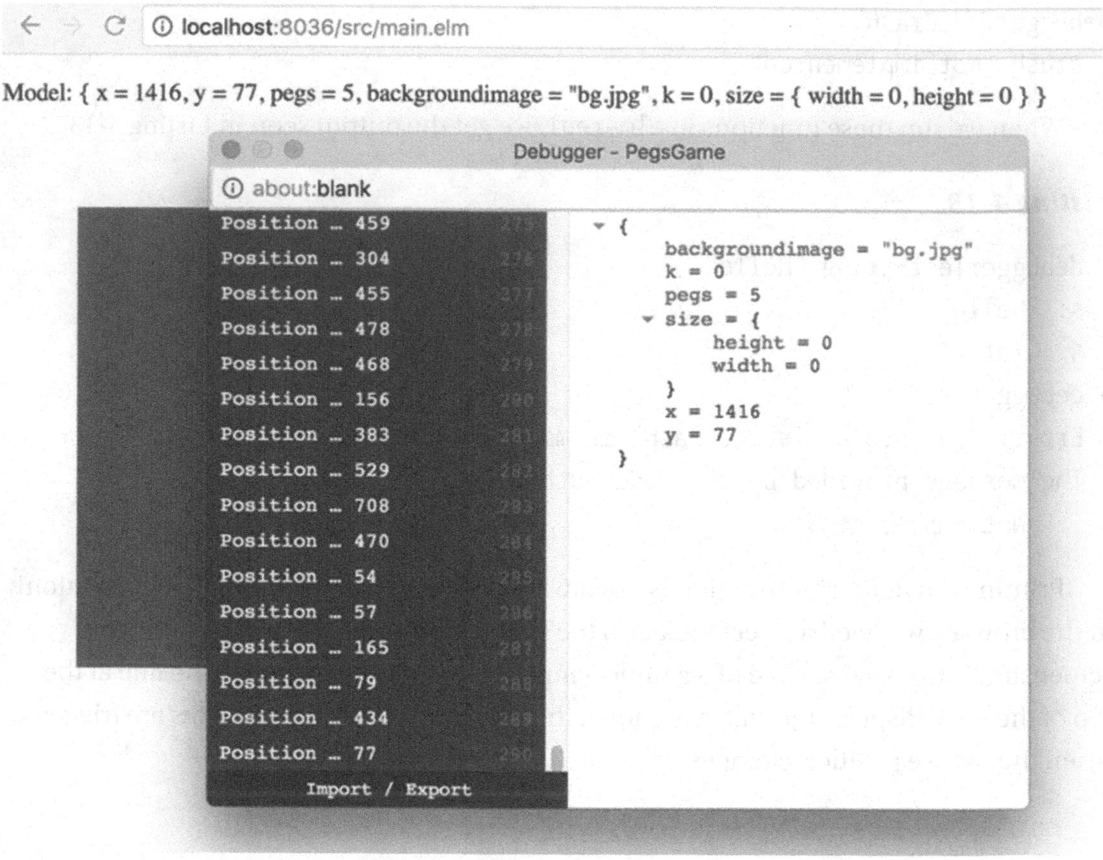

← → C ⓘ **localhost**:8036/src/main.elm

Model: { x = 1416, y = 77, pegs = 5, backgroundimage = "bg.jpg", k = 0, size = { width = 0, height = 0 } }

Figure 4-2. *Elm reactor debugger*

The overlay window titled *Debugger* shows the state changes as well. The difference is that we can export all the states to a file and import one for later use to bring the application into the exact state we want to show—perhaps an error state. We can also click on one state change and resume from there.

Debugging Elm applications is not easy. We hope to get more tools in the future as the Elm platform evolves.

Standard Libraries

A programming language is only one part of a platform. Without tools and libraries it is very difficult if not impossible to create applications in a productive way. The Elm platform is geared toward web applications, so it is no surprise that many packages created with the Elm language are handling exactly this task.

This section is titled "Standard Libraries," so a developer coming from other languages may think that there is one module that includes what may be called a standard library. Due to the platform being in development, there are a few places to look for such a library.

The following diagram (Figure 4-3) has an overview of the packages I am considering as constituting a first version of the Elm standard library.

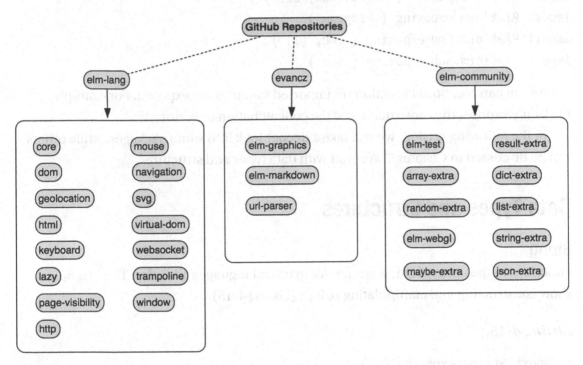

Figure 4-3. *Elm standard library*

There are more packages in the mentioned repositories, as the diagram only shows the most important and also the regularly updated packages. Some of the packages from other repositories might transit into the *official* elm-lang repository in later Elm platform versions.

The packages shown in Listing 4-14 are imported by default; therefore, no implicit import statement is necessary.

Listing 4-14.

```
import Basics exposing (..)
import Debug
import List exposing ( List, (::) )
import Maybe exposing ( Maybe( Just, Nothing ) )
import Result exposing ( Result( Ok, Err ) )
import Platform exposing ( Program )
import Platform.Cmd exposing ( Cmd, (!) )
import Platform.Sub exposing ( Sub )
```

As you can see, not all functions of imported modules are exposed. For example, List only exposes the constructor and the concatenation operator ::.

In the following section, we will take a deeper look into some packages, while others will be discussed in Chapter 5. We start with data types and structures.

Data Types and Structures

String

Functions in the library String are similar to other languages' libraries. The examples show constructing and manipulating strings (Listing 4-15).

Listing 4-15.

```
> import String exposing (..)
> reverse "Calzone"
  "enozlaC" : String
> length "Calzone"
  7 : Int
> repeat 5 "C"
  "CCCCC" : String
> isEmpty ""
  True : Bool
> cons 'C' "alzone"
  "Calzone" : String
> uncons "CCalzone"
  Just ('C',"Calzone") : Maybe.Maybe ( Char, String )
```

```
> fromChar 'C'
  "C" : String
> append "C" "alzone"
  "Calzone" : String
> concat ["C","alzone"]
  "Calzone" : String
> split "/" "Calzone/Margherita"
  ["Calzone","Margherita"] : List String
> join "/" ["Calzone","Margherita"]
  "Calzone/Margherita" : String
> words "Calzone Margherita / QuatroStagione"
  ["Calzone","Margherita","/","QuatroStagione"] : List String
> lines "Calzone\nMargherita"
  ["Calzone","Margherita"] : List String
```

Most examples are easy to understand. Interesting are cons and uncons. The first function constructs a new string by adding a character to the beginning of a string. The signature is Char ➤ String ➤ String, so it is not possible to add a character type at the end. The string can be empty, but the character must be valid, although it can be a space. A space and an empty string create a string with a blank (Listing 4-16).

Listing 4-16.

```
> import String exposing (..)
> cons ' ' ""
  " " : String
```

The function uncons splits a string into a head and a tail, where the head is a character. The result is a Maybe. A non-empty string will return a tuple of type Just with a character and a string. If we have only one element in a string as in the following example the tuple will still have two elements. An empty string will return Nothing. See Listing 4-17.

Listing 4-17.

```
> import String exposing (..)
> uncons ""
  Nothing : Maybe.Maybe ( Char, String )
> uncons "1"
  Just ('1',"") : Maybe.Maybe ( Char, String )
```

This function is useful for pattern matching; for example, to capitalize a string as in the community package `string-extra`. Listing 4-18 shows the code from the community package.

Listing 4-18.

```
{-| Change the case of the first letter of a string to either uppercase or
lowercase, depending of the value of `wantedCase`. This is an internal
function for use in `toSentenceCase` and `decapitalize`.
-}
changeCase : (Char -> Char) -> String -> String
changeCase mutator word =
    uncons word
        |> Maybe.map (\( head, tail ) -> (cons (mutator head) tail))
        |> Maybe.withDefault ""

toSentenceCase : String -> String
toSentenceCase word =
    changeCase (toUpper) word
```

When we run `toSentenceCase` it will change the first character no matter how many words are in the string. The private function `changeCase`—it is not exported—uses `uncons` on the string we pass in to get head and tail. Then, it uses `cons` to create a new string with the changed head character and the tail. If the passed-in string (`word`) is empty it returns an empty string as well, defined by the default value for `Maybe`.

We have encountered `Maybe` before and will learn later in this chapter what `Maybe` functions like `map` and `default` can do.

Listing 4-19 shows the output of `toSentenceCase` with different arguments.

Listing 4-19.

```
> toSentenceCase "first"
  "First" : String
> toSentenceCase "FIRST"
  "FIRST" : String
> toSentenceCase "First"
  "First" : String
> toSentenceCase "first word"
  "First word" : String
```

Programs often have to process strings by slicing them or searching to see whether other strings are contained within them. The String library has the usual functions to achieve these tasks. Some names may be a bit different, like dropLeft and dropRight. As in other languages, string indexes start with 0. See Listing 4-20.

Listing 4-20.

```
> slice -3 7  "Calzone"
  "one" : String
> left 3 "Calzone"
  "Cal" : String
> right 3 "Calzone"
  "one" : String
> dropLeft 4 "Calzone"
  "one" : String
> dropRight 3 "Calzone"
  "Calz" : String
> contains "one" "Calzone"
  True : Bool
> startsWith "one" "Calzone"
  False : Bool
> endsWith "one" "Calzone"
  True : Bool
> indexes "one" "Calzone"
  [4] : List Int
```

String conversions like trim or pad work in Elm as expected. Type conversions like toInt and toFloat are interesting (Listing 4-21).

Listing 4-21.

```
> toInt "1"
  Ok 1 : Result.Result String Int
> toInt "C"
  Err "could not convert string 'C' to an Int" : Result.Result String Int
> Result.withDefault 0 (toInt "C")
  0 : Int
```

```
> String.toFloat "1"
  Ok 1 : Result.Result String Float
> toList "Calzone"
  ['C','a','l','z','o','n','e'] : List Char
> fromList ['C','a','l','z','o','n','e']
  "Calzone" : String
> toUpper "Calzone"
  "CALZONE" : String
> toLower "CALZONE"
  "calzone" : String
> pad 10 '-' "Calzone"
  "--Calzone-" : String
> padLeft 10 '-' "Calzone"
  "---Calzone" : String
> padRight 10 '-' "Calzone"
  "Calzone---" : String
> trim "    Calzone"
  "Calzone" : String
> trim "    Calzone    "
  "Calzone" : String
> trimLeft "    Calzone    "
  "Calzone    " : String
> trimRight "    Calzone    "
  "    Calzone" : String
```

Type conversions return a Result type, which we will also mention later in the section about Maybe. Other languages may throw an exception or return null or some arbitrary code like -1. Returning a type like Return that can be pattern matched improves the code. If the result is correct it returns an Ok value, with the value having a type like int or float.

To avoid having to deal with Ok and Err we can use Result.withDefault, provide a default value like 0 in the preceding example, and get a value of the type we wanted returned. Of course, by using this method we would fall back to some arbitrary value to indicate failure.

Strings in Elm can also be manipulated with higher-order functions, as in the following code snippet (Listing 4-22). Those functions like map look like the list counterparts we will discuss in the next section and remind us again that strings are actually implemented as lists.

Listing 4-22.

```
-- allbasics.elm
charToUpper : Char -> String -> String
charToUpper c s =
  s ++ (fromChar c |> toUpper)

-- elm-repl
> filter (\c -> c == 'z') "Calzone"
  "z" : String
> map (\c -> if c == 'z' || c == 'n'  then '?' else c) "Calzone"
  "Cal?o?e" : String
> any (\c -> c == 'z') "Calzone"
  True : Bool
> all (\c -> c == 'z') "Calzone"
  False : Bool
> foldl charToUpper "" "Calzone"
  "CALZONE" : String
> foldr charToUpper "" "Calzone"
  "ENOZLAC" : String
```

We define a function charToUpper that takes a character and a string, converts the character to an uppercase string, and appends it to the string we provide as argument. The fromChar c |> toUpper expression has to convert the character to a string first, because toUpper has a string as input. The function fromChar is defined in the library String.

The Elm String library has—as other functional languages and libraries do—*fold* functions, also known as *reduce* functions, *aggregate* functions, or similar. These functions take as arguments a function to process each element, a start data structure (also called an accumulator), and the data structure that should be processed. In our case, accumulator and default data are strings, and the processing function is the aforementioned charToUpper. We can use them to process the string from the left or right side, so foldr charToUpper "" "Calzone" will return "ENOZLAC".

The other examples in the preceding listing also take functions to process the string we pass in. We are using anonymous functions or lambdas to define the processing functions for `filter` and `map`. The functions any and `all` take lambdas as well, but they are commonly called predicates.

List

Lists, in particular ones implemented as linked lists, are used often in functional languages. LISP or Scheme are obvious examples. Developers programming with imperative languages also use lists, although arrays that have random access to elements are sometimes preferred.

The Elm library `List` has many functions we are used to from other languages. The examples in Listing 4-23 mostly use strings as list elements.

Listing 4-23.

```
> List.isEmpty ["C","a","l","z","o","n","e"]
  False : Bool
> List.length ["C","a","l","z","o","n","e"]
  7 : Int
> List.reverse ["C","a","l","z","o","n","e"]
  ["e","n","o","z","l","a","C"] : List String
> member "o" ["C","a","l","z","o","n","e"]
  True : Bool
> range 2 10
  [2,3,4,5,6,7,8,9,10] : List Int
> List.repeat 5 "C"
  ["C","C","C","C","C"] : List String
> "C" :: ["a","l","z","o","n","e"]
  ["C","a","l","z","o","n","e"] : List String
> List.append ["C","a","l"] ["z","o","n","e"]
  ["C","a","l","z","o","n","e"] : List String
> List.concat [["C","a","l"],["z","o","n","e"]]
  ["C","a","l","z","o","n","e"] : List String
> intersperse "and" ["Calzone","Margherita"]
  ["Calzone","and","Margherita"] : List String
> intersperse "/" (List.concat [["C","a","l"],["z","o","n","e"]])
  ["C","/","a","/","l","/","z","/","o","/","n","/","e"] : List String
```

One function that deals with integers is range, which takes two integers as start and end values and returns a list with the range specified. If end is greater than start an empty list is returned.

The functions append and concat both create one list from the passed-in arguments. The difference is that append takes exactly two lists and concat takes a list of lists to put into one list. The function intersperse puts a specified string between all members of the provided list.

Tip   You may have noticed that sometimes we use the fully qualified name for functions. This is, for example, true for functions in the libraries List and String because they have the same name. If you import List, exposing everything, then no namespace needs to be used, but if you have the library String imported as well, you need to use the fully qualified name. If you import and expose exactly the functions from the libraries you want to use then you could avoid name conflicts.

The most important tasks for dealing with lists are sorting and searching. Before that, we may need to split lists into sublists with fewer elements. The head and tail functions shown in the example in Listing 4-24 are important for the implementation of recursive algorithms. The functions take and drop create sublists for further processing.

Listing 4-24.

```
> head ["C","a","1","z","o","n","e"]
  Just "C" : Maybe.Maybe String
> tail ["C","a","1","z","o","n","e"]
  Just ["a","1","z","o","n","e"] : Maybe.Maybe (List String)
> take 4 ["C","a","1","z","o","n","e"]
  ["C","a","1","z"] : List String
> drop 4 ["C","a","1","z","o","n","e"]
  ["o","n","e"] : List String
> sort ["C","a","1","z","o","n","e"]
  ["C","a","e","1","n","o","z"] : List String
> unzip [("Calzone",5),("Margherita",2)]
  (["Calzone","Margherita"],[5,2]) : ( List String, List number )
```

With sort we can process lists of *comparable* elements like strings or numbers. If we want to write our own comparison function we can use sortWith as in Listing 4-25.

The following examples also show functions that work on all elements of a list, similar to a for-each loop in imperative languages, mostly fold and map functions.

Listing 4-25.

```
> List.filter (\s -> s == "z") ["C","a","l","z","o","n","e"]
  ["z"] : List String
> sortBy String.toLower ["C","a","l","z","o","n","e"]
  ["a","C","e","l","n","o","z"] : List String
> partition (\s -> s > "n") ["C","a","l","z","o","n","e"]
  (["z","o"],["C","a","l","n","e"]) : ( List String, List String )
> List.map (\s -> toUpper s) ["C","a","l","z","o","n","e"]
  ["C","A","L","Z","O","N","E"] : List String
> List.map2 (++) ["C","a","l","z"] ["o","n","e"]
  ["Co","an","le"] : List String
> List.map2 (*) [4,5,10] [2,2,2]
  [8,10,20] : List number
> filterMap (\n -> if n > 21 then Just n else Nothing) [5,56,13,2,49]
  [56,49] : List number
> List.indexedMap (,) ["Calzone","Margherita","Quattro Stagione"]
  [(0,"Calzone"),(1,"Margherita"),(2,"Quattro Stagione")] : List ( Int,
  String )
> List.foldl (::) [] ["C","a","l","z","o","n","e"]
  ["e","n","o","z","l","a","C"] : List String
> List.foldr (::) [] ["C","a","l","z","o","n","e"]
  ["C","a","l","z","o","n","e"] : List String
> sum [5,56,13,2,49]
  125 : number
> product [5,56,13,2,49]
  356720 : number
> maximum ["C","a","l","z","o","n","e"]
  Just "z" : Maybe.Maybe String
> minimum ["C","a","l","z","o","n","e"]
  Just "C" : Maybe.Maybe String
```

```
> List.all (\s -> s > "a") ["C","a","1","z","o","n","e"]
  False : Bool
> List.any (\s -> s > "a") ["C","a","1","z","o","n","e"]
  True : Bool
> scanl (::) [] ["C","a","1","z","o","n","e"]
  [[],["C"],["a","C"],["1","a","C"],["z","1","a","C"],["o","z","1","a","C"],
  ["n","o","z","1","a","C"],["e","n","o","z","1","a","C"]]
    : List (List String)
> sortWith (\s1 s2 -> GT) ["C","a","1","z","o","n","e"]
  ["e","n","o","z","1","a","C"] : List String
> concatMap (\s -> s :: ["o"]) ["C","a","1","z","o","n","e"]
  ["C","o","a","o","1","o","z","o","o","o","n","o","e","o"] : List String
```

The map function with a number shows how many lists can be passed as arguments. One argument means that all elements of one list will be processed, while more arguments mean that all lists will be combined by applying the passed-in function to the elements of the list and then creating one resulting list.

Interesting are functions like maximum or sum that use mapping functions to provide predefined tasks. It is also worth noting that some of these functions always return a result, others sometimes a Maybe. For example, sum, with an empty list passed in, will return 0. The function minimum does not have a default value, so it has to return a Maybe if an empty list is passed in. If elements are not comparable, the compilation of the code will fail.

The functions all and any invoke a function that is passed as an argument to all elements and behave like logical and or. Either all elements (and) or any element (or) of a list return true for the predicate function and thus return true for the whole list.

Lists are the base for the implementation of other data structures, as we will see in the following sections.

Array

Arrays are similar to lists, with the big advantage that due to their implementation elements can be accessed via indices. The Elm platform uses a tree implementation, while other language libraries—for example .Net—use arrays as implementation for a data structure that is called list.

The similarity to lists can be seen when we look at the functions in the library that are almost the same compared to List, with the big exception of manipulating arrays with indices. See Listing 4-26.

Listing 4-26.

```
> empty
  Array.fromList [] : Array.Array a
> Array.repeat 5 "C"
  Array.fromList ["C","C","C","C","C"] : Array.Array String
> initialize 5 (\s -> "C")
  Array.fromList ["C","C","C","C","C"] : Array.Array String
> arr = Array.fromList ["C","a","l","z","o","n","e"]
  Array.fromList ["C","a","l","z","o","n","e"] : Array.Array String
> Array.isEmpty arr
  False : Bool
> Array.length arr
  7 : Int
> push "5" arr
  Array.fromList ["C","a","l","z","o","n","e","5"] : Array.Array String
> Array.append (Array.fromList ["Calzone"]) (Array.fromList ["Margeritha"])
  Array.fromList ["Calzone","Margeritha"] : Array.Array String
> Array.toList arr
  ["C","a","l","z","o","n","e"] : List String
> toIndexedList arr
  [(0,"C"),(1,"a"),(2,"l"),(3,"z"),(4,"o"),(5,"n"),(6,"e")]
    : List ( Int, String )
> get 0 arr
  Just "C" : Maybe.Maybe String
> arr2 = Array.set 0 "Hawai" arr
  Array.fromList ["Hawai"] : Array.Array String
> get 0 arr
  Just "C" : Maybe.Maybe String
> get 0 arr2
  Just "Hawai" : Maybe.Maybe String
```

```
> arr3 = Array.set 2 "Hawai" arr
  Array.fromList ["C"] : Array.Array String
> get 3 arr
  Nothing : Maybe.Maybe String
```

We create arrays from lists directly or use functions like `initialize`. Once we have an array, we can manipulate it with `append`, but we also have functions that work with inidices.

The functions get and `set` expect as arguments an index number. Both work with indices out of range and do not throw a runtime error, as we know from other programming languages. The behavior of `set` is a bit unusual because it returns the original array and assigns it, although there was clearly something else intended. The array `arr3` in the preceding example tries to manipulate the array `arr` and passes the number 2 as the argument. The returned array is the original `arr`.

If we pass a wrong index to get we receive `Nothing` as this function always returns a Maybe.

Other manipulation functions return parts of an array. See Listing 4-27.

Listing 4-27.

```
> arr = Array.fromList ["C","a","l","z","o","n","e"]
  Array.fromList ["C","a","l","z","o","n","e"] : Array.Array String
> Array.slice 0 4 arr
  Array.fromList ["C","a","l","z"] : Array.Array String
> Array.slice -3 7 arr
  Array.fromList ["o","n","e"] : Array.Array String
```

The function `slice` takes start and end indices, where the end index is not included in the result. Even the start can be negative, which requires a little brain acrobatics to figure out the expected result. See Listing 4-28.

Listing 4-28.

```
> arr = Array.fromList ["C","a","l","z","o","n","e"]
  Array.fromList ["C","a","l","z","o","n","e"] : Array.Array String
> Array.map (\e -> String.toUpper e) arr
  Array.fromList ["C","A","L","Z","O","N","E"] : Array.Array String
```

```
> Array.filter (\e -> e > "n") arr
  Array.fromList ["z","o"] : Array.Array String
> Array.foldl (\e l -> String.toUpper e :: l) [] arr
  ["E","N","O","Z","L","A","C"] : List String
> Array.foldr (\e l -> String.toUpper e :: l) [] arr
  ["C","A","L","Z","O","N","E"] : List String
> Array.indexedMap (*) (Array.fromList [11,22,31])
  Array.fromList [0,22,62] : Array.Array Int
> Array.indexedMap (+) (Array.fromList [11,22,31])
  Array.fromList [11,23,33] : Array.Array Int
```

Arrays can also be manipulated with functions that are known from List, like map or fold. IndexedMap needs a bit more information because it is not immediately obvious what is happening. The function takes a lambda—in our case, multiplication—and creates another array by applying the function to the index of an element and its value. The first index is 0, so the multiplication returns 0 as well. If we pass addition as the manipulation function we get as the first value the elements' value of 11 plus 0.

We used simple functions in our examples, but with more sophisticated functions it is possible, for example, to create an array of tuples or other similar data structures. Of course, this only makes sense if the index numbers of the array's elements contain information about the elements.

Dict

Dictionaries are used to create key–value pairs. Other languages might call them *hashes* or similar. They all store keys of one type and relate them to values of one type. The elements are unordered and are accessed via keys. In Elm all keys must be of the type comparable. See Listing 4-29.

Listing 4-29.

```
> Dict.empty
  Dict.fromList [] : Dict.Dict k v
> d = singleton "Margherita" 3
  Dict.fromList [("Margherita",3)] : Dict.Dict String number
> Dict.fromList [("Calzone",8),("Calzone",4)]
  Dict.fromList [("Calzone",4)] : Dict.Dict String number
```

```
> insert "Calzone" 12 d
  Dict.fromList [("Calzone",12)] : Dict.Dict String number
> update "Calzone" (\v -> Just 12) d
  Dict.fromList [("Calzone",12)] : Dict.Dict String number
> remove "Calzone" d
  Dict.fromList [] : Dict.Dict String number
> Dict.isEmpty d
  False : Bool
> Dict.member "Calzone" d
  True : Bool
> Dict.get "Margherita" ds
  Just 3 : Maybe.Maybe number
> Dict.get "Calzone" ds
  Nothing : Maybe.Maybe number
```

As is the case with other data structures, dictionaries are based on Elm's list implementation. This is why we see as the result of almost all functions in our examples Dict.fromList. Most functions in Dict are straightforward to understand. A bit surprising is the name of the function singleton, which creates a dictionary with a single key–value pair. Our minds are used to thinking of the pattern Singleton, which is used to create only a single instance of a type.

We see that internally dictionaries are lists of tuples, with one tuple consisting of two elements—key and value. This internal representation is transparent for the user because most functions take simple type arguments. Only if we want to use Dict. fromList ourselves will we have to create a list of tuples.

When we update a dictionary, we pass the key and a function that checks the value of the pair element: (-> Just 12). It needs to match against a Maybe because, again, there is possibly no default value defined. See Listing 4-30.

Listing 4-30.

```
> d = Dict.fromList [("Calzone",8),("Margherita",4)]
  Dict.fromList [("Calzone",8),("Margherita",4)] : Dict.Dict String number
> ds = singleton "Quattro Stagione" 0
  Dict.fromList [("Quattro Stagione",0)] : Dict.Dict String number
> Dict.toList d
  [("Calzone",8),("Margherita",4)] : List ( String, number )
```

111

```
> keys d
  ["Calzone","Margherita"] : List String
> values d
  [8,4] : List number
> union d ds
  Dict.fromList [("Calzone",8),("Margherita",4),("Quattro Stagione",0)]
    : Dict.Dict String number
> diff d (Dict.fromList [("Calzone",6),("Quattro Stagione",1 )])
  Dict.fromList [("Margherita",4)] : Dict.Dict String number
> intersect d (Dict.fromList [("Calzone",6),("Quattro Stagione",1 )])
  Dict.fromList [("Calzone",8)] : Dict.Dict String number
```

With the functions union, diff, and intersect we can create a dict from dicts. Important to know is that in the functions union and intersect the preference is given to the first dict. The preceding example shows that there are the same keys but with different values in the dicts we pass as arguments. The resulting dict contains the element with the value of the first dict. This may lead to difficult-to-find errors when the order of the dict arguments is not guaranteed.

The following examples show the fold and map functions we have seen in other data structures as well, and they work in the same manner. However, map does not return the original values of a key–value pair, but rather a pair of the key and a Boolean value indicating if the mapping function that works on the value succeeded or not. See Listing 4-31.

Listing 4-31.

```
> d = Dict.fromList [("Calzone",8),("Margherita",4)]
  Dict.fromList [("Calzone",8),("Margherita",4)] : Dict.Dict String number
> Dict.map (\k v -> v < 5) d
  Dict.fromList [("Calzone",False),("Margherita",True)] : Dict.Dict String Bool
> Dict.partition (\k v -> v < 5) d
  (Dict.fromList [("Margherita",4)],Dict.fromList [("Calzone",8)])
    : ( Dict.Dict String number, Dict.Dict String number )
> Dict.partition (\k v -> v < 3) d
  (Dict.fromList [],Dict.fromList [("Calzone",8),("Margherita",4)])
    : ( Dict.Dict String number, Dict.Dict String number )
```

```
> Dict.filter (\k v -> v < 5) d
  Dict.fromList [("Margherita",4)] : Dict.Dict String number
> Dict.filter (\k v -> k < "F") d
  Dict.fromList [("Calzone",8)] : Dict.Dict String number
> Dict.foldl (\k v acc -> acc ++ String.toUpper k) "" d
  "CALZONEMARGHERITA" : String
> Dict.foldr (\k v acc -> acc ++ String.toUpper k) "" d
  "MARGHERITACALZONE" : String
> Dict.foldl (\k v acc -> acc + v) 0 d
  12 : number
> Dict.foldr (\k v acc -> acc + v) 0 d
  12 : number
```

A special map function is `partition`, which applies a predicate to all elements and keeps the one that returns true in one dict and the rest in another dict. Both dicts are returned in a tuple.

Set

Sets are similar to lists, but their values must be unique. We can create a set from a list, although duplicates will be removed to keep the values unique. Elements of sets are comparables, and when we create from a list the elements will also be ordered.

In Listing 4-32 we define a set with the name s2 from a list of strings. Note that one duplicate element is removed, and the rest is ordered. The set with the name s1 is created from a tuple, which is a comparable as well.

Listing 4-32.

```
> Set.empty
  Set.fromList [] : Set.Set a
> Set.fromList ["Margherita", "Margherita", "Calzone"]
  Set.fromList ["Calzone","Margherita"] : Set.Set String
> st = singleton "Calzone"
  Set.fromList ["Calzone"] : Set.Set String
> s = Set.fromList ["Calzone","Margherita"]
  Set.fromList ["Calzone","Margherita"] : Set.Set String
```

```
> Set.singleton ("Quattro Stagione", 5)
  Set.fromList [("Quattro Stagione",5)] : Set.Set ( String, number )
> Set.size s
  2 : Int
> Set.isEmpty s
  False : Bool
> f = Set.member "Calzone"
  <function> : Set.Set String -> Bool
> f s
  True : Bool
> Set.toList s
  ["Calzone","Margherita"] : List String
> s1 = insert (0, "Element 1") empty
  Set.fromList [(0,"Element 1")] : Set.Set ( number, String )
> s1
  Set.fromList [(0,"Element 1")] : Set.Set ( number, String )
> s2 = Set.fromList ["Margherita", "Margherita", "Calzone"]
  Set.fromList ["Calzone","Margherita"] : Set.Set String
```

As we have seen in other data structures, almost every function in Set uses fromList to achieve its tasks. Also, if we want to see what the set with the name s1 is, we again get a fromList with a tuple list. See Listing 4-33.

Listing 4-33.

```
> s = Set.fromList ["Calzone","Margherita"]
  Set.fromList ["Calzone","Margherita"] : Set.Set String
> Set.insert ("Quattro Stagione") s
  Set.fromList ["Calzone","Margherita","Quattro Stagione"] : Set.Set String
> Set.remove "Calzone" s
  Set.fromList ["Margherita"] : Set.Set String
> Set.union s (Set.fromList ["QuattroStagione"])
  Set.fromList ["Calzone","Margherita","QuattroStagione"] : Set.Set String
> Set.union s (Set.fromList ["QuattroStagione","Calzone"])
  Set.fromList ["Calzone","Margherita","QuattroStagione"] : Set.Set String
```

```
> Set.intersect s (Set.fromList ["QuattroStagione","Calzone"])
  Set.fromList ["Calzone"] : Set.Set String
> Set.diff s (Set.fromList ["QuattroStagione","Calzone"])
  Set.fromList ["Margherita"] : Set.Set String
```

Sets have all the functions we have seen already, and these functions work in almost the same way. If we pass to union sets with the same element, only one will appear in the returned set to adhere to the uniqueness requirement of sets.

Also, functions like map, fold, and partition are available in Set and work like their counterparts in other data structures, as we can see in Listing 4-34.

Listing 4-34.

```
> s = Set.fromList ["Calzone","Margherita"]
  Set.fromList ["Calzone","Margherita"] : Set.Set String
> Set.map (\e -> String.toUpper e)  s
  Set.fromList ["CALZONE","MARGHERITA"] : Set.Set String
> Set.filter (\e -> e < "F") s
  Set.fromList ["Calzone"] : Set.Set String
> Set.partition (\e -> e < "F") s
  (Set.fromList ["Calzone"],Set.fromList ["Margherita"])
    : ( Set.Set String, Set.Set String )
> Set.foldl (\e1 e2 -> (String.toUpper e1) ++ " " ++ e2) "" s
  "MARGHERITA CALZONE " : String
> Set.foldr (\e1 e2 -> (String.toUpper e1) ++ " " ++ e2) "" s
  "CALZONE MARGHERITA " : String
```

This concludes the discussion of basic data structures in Elm. Additional functions for these data structures can be found in elm-community packages; for example, list-extra has more than 80 functions that cover all aspects of list creation and manipulation. If the vanilla functions are not sufficient, it is a good idea to look into the elm-community packages.

Revisiting Maybe

We have seen Maybe a few times now, but have never defined it properly. It is used for values that may or may not exist and is similar to null in other languages, but not quite the same. Maybe—itself a union type—wraps the value of a type and returns well-defined tags.

Maybe is useful when we define arguments we don't need or when we don't know if there is a valid value in an argument. See Listing 4-35.

Listing 4-35.

```
getPizzaFromString : String -> Maybe Pizza
getPizzaFromString p =
  case p of
    "Calzone"
      -> Just Calzone
    "Margherita"
      -> Just Margherita
    "Quattro Stagione"
      -> Just QuattroStagione

    _
      -> Nothing
```

The function getPizzaFromString can't reliably return a value of type Pizza because it does not know what the input string contains. This function implements the factory pattern[8] in a simple way. If the input is not known to the function it returns Nothing. See Listing 4-36.

Listing 4-36.

```
> getPizzaFromString "Calzone"
  Just Calzone : Maybe.Maybe AllBasics.Pizza
> getPizzaFromString ""
  Nothing : Maybe.Maybe AllBasics.Pizza
> getPizzaFromString "Unknown Pizza"
  Nothing : Maybe.Maybe AllBasics.Pizza
```

So, how do we get the value of a Maybe? Apart from pattern matching, as in the examples in the previous chapter, we can use the helper function withDefault (Listing 4-37).

---

[8]https://en.wikipedia.org/wiki/Factory_method_pattern

Listing 4-37.

```
-- type Pizza = Calzone | Margherita | QuattroStagione | UnknownPizza
> Maybe.withDefault UnknownPizza (getPizzaFromString "")
  UnknownPizza : AllBasics.Pizza
> Maybe.withDefault UnknownPizza (getPizzaFromString "Pizza with no name")
  UnknownPizza : AllBasics.Pizza
```

We are using the type Pizza as in our previous examples. Note that we have defined a tag UnknownPizza that will indicate an invalid value, similar to what Maybe defines with Nothing. Whatever we then throw at getPizzaFromString it will handle it and return Nothing. The function withDefault lets us define a default value that is returned in case of Nothing; in our case, that is UnknownPizza. This gives us a direct value without having to deal with Just and Nothing.

Sometimes we want to apply a function to a Maybe result. The example in Listing 4-38 applies the function choosePizza on a result of the function firstPizza and then returns the result as a string with the help of withDefault.

Listing 4-38.

```
> Maybe.withDefault "UnknownPizza" \
    (Maybe.map choosePizza (firstPizza [Calzone, Margherita]))
  "Pizza chosen: Calzone" : String
> Maybe.withDefault "UnknownPizza" (Maybe.map choosePizza (firstPizza []))
  "UnknownPizza" : String
```

What is happening here? Let's dissect the preceding one-liners. Listing 4-39 displays the signatures of relevant functions to follow the explanation easier.

Listing 4-39.

```
-- firstPizza : List Pizza -> Maybe Pizza
> firstPizza [Calzone, Margherita]
  Just Calzone : Maybe.Maybe AllBasics.Pizza
-- choosePizzaIf : Pizza -> String
-- Maybe.map : (a -> b) -> Maybe a -> Maybe b
> Maybe.map choosePizza (firstPizza [Calzone, Margherita])
  Just "Pizza chosen: Calzone" : Maybe.Maybe String
```

The function firstPizza returns a Maybe. This is necessary because the passed-in list could be empty, and there is no first element in the list. The function choosePizza takes a type Pizza as argument, so we need to use map to apply the function to the previous result. Of course, the previous result is a Maybe type, and the mapped function does not know anything about that type, so the mapping function only has to apply choosePizza to a valid Just value. In any case, the result is another Maybe—in this case a Maybe String—and we need to resolve with withDefault to get the string value we want.

The example could be enhanced by using partial functions. Note that parentheses are necessary to tell the compiler what we intend to do. Without this we would get compiler errors about the number of arguments. See Listing 4-40.

Listing 4-40.

```
> mapChoosePizza = Maybe.map choosePizza
  <function> : Maybe.Maybe AllBasics.Pizza -> Maybe.Maybe String
> defaultUnknownPizza = Maybe.withDefault "UnknownPizza"
  <function> : Maybe.Maybe String -> String
> defaultUnknownPizza (mapChoosePizza (firstPizza [Calzone, Margherita]))
  "Pizza chosen: Calzone" : String
```

The purpose of Maybe is to prevent null exceptions as we know them from other programming languages. What it does not reduce are the checks for valid values. Once a Maybe is in a function pipeline, this type is propagated until it can be resolved. A similar type in Elm core is Result, which is used for computational functions and returns either Ok with a value or Err with an error message.

JSON

So far we have discussed basic data types that exist in the standard library. When we create a web app, sooner or later we will run into the situation where we want to exchange data with JavaScript code or with external servers. The way to do this is to communicate via JSON objects.

Elm has Json.Encode and Json.Decode libraries to handle conversions of models into JSON and back. They are not the easiest libraries to understand, but once you have done some work with them they will be easier to handle. The community has created helper functions to deal especially with decoding on a higher level.

The following code defines two types, with Event embedded in the model as a list. We create an instance of Event and then create an instance of Model (Listing 4-41).

Listing 4-41.

```
type alias Event =
  { timestamp: Int
  , eventname: String
  }

type alias Model  =
  { xpos : Int
  , ypos : Int
  , numbertones: Int
  , backgroundimage: String
  , events: List Event
  }

ev = {timestamp = 12345, eventname = "eventname"}
m = { xpos = 0, ypos = 0, numbertones = 1,
  backgroundimage = "bg.png", events = [ev]}

> o = [("xpos",Json.Encode.int m.xpos)]
  [("xpos",0)] : List ( String, Json.Encode.Value )
> j = encode 0 (object o)
  "{\"xpos\":0}" : String
> decodeString (field "xpos" Json.Decode.int) j
  Ok 0 : Result.Result String Int
```

Once we have defined the data we can start encoding some or all fields of a type. There are two JSON packages, and for encoding we use JSON.Encode. In the expression [("xpos",Json.Encode.int m.xpos)] we create a list with one tuple—in fact, a dict. The key is the name of the field "xpos", and for the value we are interested in the field xpos in the model instance m.

Applying encode 0 (object o) then returns the JSON string from the list we just created.

The other way to extract a value from a JSON string involves methods in `JSON.Decode`. In the preceding example we use `decodeString`—`string` means we are decoding a string—and extract the value of type `int` we previously encoded. The method returns a `Result` type to indicate success or failure.

This is just a short introduction to the JSON libraries. As you can see, it is not straightforward to use them. We will encounter JSON processing much more in Chapter 6 when we discuss a full example of a web application with Elm.

What We Learned

This chapter introduced us to the built-in REPL, and we looked at the development process and the tools in the Elm platform that support us. The overview of library packages was just that, an overview, but hopefully it gave you an idea of the power of the Elm platform.

In the next chapter, we will learn about the Elm architecture and more standard libraries that support this architecture.

CHAPTER 5

Elm Architecture and Building Blocks

This chapter is about the *Elm architecture*, which is the standard way to create applications with the Elm platform. We will learn what this architecture pattern is, how we can implement it, and how our code can be organized for easy development and maintenance.

Once we understand the architecture, we can look at building blocks, like styling or HTTP requests, we can use to create our applications.

Note   This chapter uses code examples from the application *PizzaOrder* we describe in the next chapter. The code can be found in the downloads for this book in the folder *PizzaOrder*.

The Elm architecture lies at the heart of the Elm platform. It is a simple but powerful architecture similar to the Model-View-Controller concept that is used in many other frameworks and platforms. The advantage of the Elm architecture is that important wiring is done in the background. This makes it a little bit difficult at first to understand what is going on, but once the concept is clear we see that it reduces code in our application significantly.

The following diagram (Figure 5-1) displays all important parts of the Elm architecture.

© Wolfgang Loder 2018
W. Loder, *Web Applications with Elm*, https://doi.org/10.1007/978-1-4842-2610-0_5

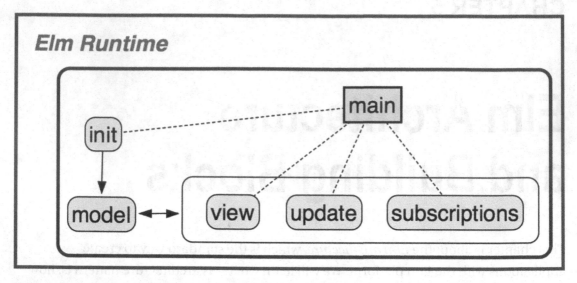

Figure 5-1. *Elm architecture overview*

The code in the inner shape is dependent on the *Elm runtime* in the outer shape. The function main is the entry point into the application and binds all parts together as in Listing 5-1.

Listing 5-1.

```
main : Program Never Model Msg
main =
  program
    { init = init
    , view = view
    , update = update
    , subscriptions = subscriptions
    }
```

Main calls a function program from the package HTML and passes key–value pairs as parameters. Key names like init are given and mandatory, but the key values— the names of our implementation functions—can be any name as far as the function signature is met. Most developers leave the function names as shown in the listing.

For example, the function init has the following type definition: init : (model, Cmd msg). It does not take any parameters and returns a tuple. We will get more into these definitions in the following paragraphs.

We pass references to the functions for `init`, `subscriptions`, `update`, and `view`. When we run our application, `main` will be invoked, and the Elm runtime will wire up the code of the application with the relevant code in the runtime. This runtime consists of JavaScript functions that are bound to our compiled code to make things work. So, we can say that the functions in `main` are callbacks that are called at certain times by the runtime.

We can define `main` as we just did, but there is one other important option. We may want to pass arguments when we start the application. In our HTML page we can have the JavaScript code shown in Listing 5-2.

Listing 5-2.

```
let elmapp = Elm.PizzaOrder.fullscreen({
    initialnumber: 10
});
```

These lines of code call the application, tell it to go full screen, and pass in one argument with the name `initialnumber` and the value 10.

To make this happen, we need to change our `main` function. Our first version has in its signature `Never`, which tells the Elm runtime to ignore the second argument to the type `Program`. So, we change the function `main` and use `programWithFlags` instead of program. See Listing 5-3.

Listing 5-3.

```
main : Program (Maybe Flags) Model Msg
main =
    programWithFlags
    { init = init
    , view = view
    , update = update
    , subscriptions = subscriptions
    }
```

We just tell the Elm runtime to expect flags. It is a `Maybe` type because the passed in JavaScript object could be empty.

123

Note   The native JavaScript code in the package `core` called `Platform.js` checks if there are flags defined or not. If we use `program` and have a flag defined we will get a runtime error in JavaScript. The same happens if we use `programWithFlags` and do not provide a flag.

We will see in the section about `init` later in this chapter how to handle flags and use them to configure our application at initialization.

Elm Architecture Overview

Let's examine all parts of the Elm architecture we have to implement to make the architecture work.

Note   The examples that follow use functions and types from the file `allbasic.elm`, which we already used in Chapter 3.

---

model

A model represents the state we use in our application. The model is passed from function to function, and its values are updated in our code. The following model is from a simple game and contains values for mouse positions (`x,y`), the name of the background image (`backgroundimage`), and the number of stones in the game (`stones`). All those values are simple types; `size`, however—indicating the dimensions of the window—uses a type `Size` that is imported from the module `Window`. See Listing 5-4.

Listing 5-4.

```
type alias Model  =
  { x : Int
  , y : Int
  , stones: Int
  , backgroundimage: String
  , size: Size
  }
```

Not all models will be as simple as this example, but many times it is sufficient. A more complicated model is shown in Listing 5-5.

Listing 5-5.

```
type alias PizzaOrder =
  { number: String
  , pizza: String
  , toppings: List String
  , size: String
  }

type alias Customer =
    { name: String
    , address: String
    , telephone: String
    , ordered: List PizzaOrder
    , selected: PizzaOrder
    , time: String
    , amount: Float
    }

type alias NestedModel  =
  { temporder: Customer
  , orders: List PizzaOrder
  , currenttime: String
  }
```

We see lists and nested types in the preceding model, which is similar to relational data models. Such models work, although code to access type fields is more complicated than for simpler models.

Before we use any of our models in an application, it is a good idea to initialize them. As always in Elm, we are using a function to achieve this; in this case, the initializing functions for both models return a constant value. See Listing 5-6.

Listing 5-6.

```
initialModel: Model
initialModel =
  { x = 0
  , y = 0
  , stones = 5
  , backgroundimage = "bg.jpg"
  , size = Size 0 0
  }

initialNestedModel : NestedModel
initialNestedModel =
  NestedModel (Customer "" "" "" []
              (PizzaOrder "1" "" [] "")
          "" 0.00)
          [] ""
```

Note   The function `initialNestedModel` was formatted to fit for printing. For a successful compilation, all parameters should be on one line, but multiple lines may work with your editor.

There are two ways available to us to create a custom type in code. As we saw in Chapter 3, these types are basically records. Therefore, we can just define keys and their values.

Another way is to use a constructor without specifying the names of keys. In this case, the order of fields must be preserved; otherwise, compiler errors will result.

The first function `initialModel` uses the more verbose form, which makes clear which key has what value. The function `initialNestedModel` uses the constructor and passes values as parameters. Nested models are separated with parentheses to indicate to the compiler which value belongs to which key.

Initialization functions are useful to initialize the model at the start of the application and give it default values.

A model can be as complicated as you like, but in practice it is better to keep it as flat as possible. Restrictions in pattern matching make the latter easier to handle, as we will see when we discuss the `update` function.

init

The init function initializes the model with the function we implemented earlier and can also invoke a command. This is a description that hides the fact that there is a lot going on in the Elm runtime when we run init.

A *command* is part of a bigger group called *effects*. It is helpful to keep in mind that effects are in fact data that tell the Elm runtime what we want to do in a declarative way. Other *data* in this group are HTML declarations and *subscriptions*. When the Elm runtime receives the effect declaration it works on it to make the *effect* real; for example, by rendering markup or calling other functions in our application.

Many times, the init function will look like Listing 5-7.

Listing 5-7.

```
init : ( Model, Cmd Msg )
init =
  (initialModel, Cmd.none)
```

We just initialize the application's model and nothing else. The call Cmd.none simply passes an empty list to the Elm runtime. As we have mentioned before, init returns a tuple of a model and a command. The message parameter Msg is defined in our code; we will see an example in the section about update.

Sometimes we want to initialize a model's key with a value that can only be obtained by running a function that reaches outside our application; for example, to a database or to the computer system we are running the application on. In our case, we want to initialize the key currenttime with the actual time the application runs (see Listing 5-8).

Listing 5-8.

```
init : ( Model, Cmd Msg )
init =
  (initialNestedModel, Task.perform CurrentTime Time.now)
```

This expression is hard to understand at first glance. The reason that it is written like this has to do with side effects.

Note   Elm is a functional language, so side effects can't be handled directly. The diagram in Figure 5-2 shows the generic concept of how Elm handles side effects.

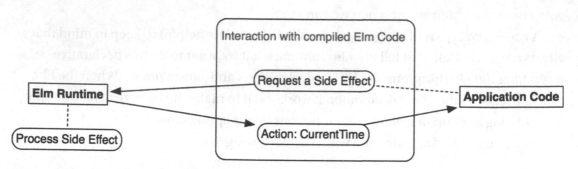

Figure 5-2. *Side Effects in Elm*

Note   Think of the Elm platform runtime—which is the JavaScript we looked at previously when we discussed the output of the Elm compiler—as code that can handle everything JavaScript can process without having any problem with side effects. The Elm application code tells the runtime that a side-effect task should be performed. The runtime processes this request and sends back an action command. The (compiled) Elm code then reacts to the command.

So, what happens in the preceding expression? We declare our intention to get the current time and create a task to perform that request. We also tell the runtime what to do once it has the result—that is, sending the command message CurrentTime. This way, the side-effect call is separated from the application and the state of the application is protected.

We have previously shown in this chapter how to use a main function with flags as the entry point into our application. The init function needs to change to handle those flags.

First, we need to change our model to be able to save our flag values. In our case, we just create a custom type Flags with one field, called initialnumber. See Listing 5-9.

Listing 5-9.

```
type alias Flags =
  { initialnumber : Int
  }

initialModel: Model
initialModel =
  { x = 0
  , y = 0
  , stones = 5
  , backgroundimage = "bg.jpg"
  , size = Size 0 0
  , flags: Flags
  }
```

We use the type `Flags` to tell Elm which types and values to expect from JavaScript. We also change the signature of the `init` function because we expect a parameter from the Elm runtime to be passed into our function. See Listing 5-10.

Listing 5-10.

```
init : Maybe Flags -> ( Model, Cmd Msg )
init flags =
  let
    initialstate =
      case flags of
        Maybe.Just flags ->
          {initialModel | flags = (Flags flags.initialnumber)}
        Nothing ->
          initialModel
  in
    (initialstate , Task.perform CurrentTime Time.now)
```

The parameter `flags` is a `Maybe` type, so we need to check if it has a value, and then we can initialize our model. If we use more than one flag, we must be sure that all flags are provided and that all flags have the right type. The compiler can't check at compile time, but the runtime will throw an error if there are mismatches like wrong types, too many, or too few flags.

Whatever we have to initialize in our application, the init function just passes data to the runtime; it does not process this data and is not called later as the application runs.

update

At the heart of the Elm architecture lies the update function. With the model we are passing not only data to our application functions, but also messages. Those messages— also called *actions* or *commands*—are implemented in the function that is passed to the update key in init, and all possible messages are declared as union types.

It is not necessary to call the message type Msg, but most applications use that name to make it easier to read the code. See Listing 5-11.

Listing 5-11.

```
type Msg
    = AddOrder
    | ConfirmOrder
    | CancelOrder
    | CurrentTime Time
    | NoOp
```

The elements of Msg look like an enumeration, but this hides that they can have parameters, as in the example CurrentTime. It is better to think of union types as members of functions. The type Msg usually declares all messages that can be passed to update.

The update function takes a message of type Msg and the Model as parameters and returns the same tuple as the init function does. An implementation looks like Listing 5-12.

Listing 5-12.

```
update : Msg -> NestedModel -> ( Model, Cmd Msg )
update msg model =
  case msg of
    NoOp ->
          (model, Cmd.none)
```

```
AddOrder ->
  let
    t = model.temporder
    to = model.temporder.ordered
    t_ = {t | ordered = t.selected :: to}
    p = toFloat ((List.length t_.ordered)) * G.SinglePrice
    m = Model {t_ | time = model.currenttime, amount = p} model.
    orders  model.currenttime
    itemlist = calculateOrder model.temporder.selected
  in
    (m, updateLists itemlist)

CurrentTime time ->
  let
    t = model.temporder
    currentplus = addMinutes (((List.length t.ordered)+1)*1)
    (fromTimestamp time)
    s = toString (DT.hour currentplus) ++ ":" ++ toString (DT.minute
    currentplus)
  in
    ({model | currenttime = s}, Cmd.none)
```

Note   Some implementation was omitted for brevity. If you try to compile the code
as it is with the type `Msg` that we discussed before, the compiler will throw errors if
not all messages are dealt with in the case expression.

The *case* expression looks for the message and runs code according to it. In
our example, we have to deal with a nested model, so the code is a little bit more
complicated. With a flat model we can just have one line and update the model with
the value we get as a parameter; in this case, we have to get the nested model and then
update.

Tip   The expression (model, Cmd.none) in the NoOp clause can be written as model ! [ ]. The infix operator ! takes a model and a list of messages and returns the tuple as needed in the update function as the return value. The advantage is that later a command can simply be added to the list without any other changes.

Some developers are implementing a catch-all clause to avoid compilation errors during development. See Listing 5-13.

Listing 5-13.

```
case msg of
  _ ->
    (model, cmd.none)
```

Make sure to delete the catch-all clause before testing for production or deploying to production to avoid difficult-to-trace errors. A better way is to use the Debug module defined in the package core. See Listing 5-14.

Listing 5-14.

```
case msg of
  _ ->
   Debug.crash "Not implemented"
```

With this line in place the application crashes and tells us that something is not (yet) implemented.

If we do not want to crash the application, we can use Debug.log with a string as the message and a value of any type. The message and the value will be printed in the developer console during runtime.

The Elm runtime calls update when one of the message types is invoked, either directly in code or in a user-interface element. If there are commands declared in the returned tuple of update it will run it; otherwise, it will pass the model to the function view.

view

The function view is the place where we declare all our markup. This function takes a model as parameter and returns a DOM element—or node—which can have other elements nested.

We do not write HTML markup in view but rather call functions like div or button. Each of these functions takes two parameters: a list of attributes and an list of nodes. See Listing 5-15.

Listing 5-15.

```
view : Model -> Html Msg
view model =
  div [class "container"] [
    div [ class "jumbotron", style [("background-color","lightblue")] ] [
      h1 [] [ text "Pizza Ordering System" ]
      , span [style [("font-size","1.4em")]] \
            [text "Example for Syncfusion Blog. First published "]
      , a [href "#", style [("font-size","1.4em")]] [text "here."]
    ]
  ]
```

This example shows a lot of information. We have a div at root level, another nested div with an h1, a span, and a link. Some of them have attributes like class or style, some call as node content the Html.text function, which takes a string as a parameter and creates a text node.

The Elm platform compiles the view function and creates markup. This process is similar to other frameworks, either server side or client side.

Note   You always need exactly one wrapper div at root level. Without it the code will not compile. It is not possible to have a list of nodes at root. The definition of the view function clearly says this, but it is easy to forget in the heat of coding.

It is easy to see that these view functions quickly get out of hand so that it is difficult to see what is going on or to see which element is nested where. We can create smaller functions for parts of the markup and compose these function in view. Listing 5-16 creates an unordered list.

Listing 5-16.

```
renderList : List PizzaOrder -> Html msg
renderList l =
  ul[]
    (List.map (\item -> li [] [ text item.pizza ]) l)
```

We get a list as the parameter, and with List.map we create for each item an li element. All these elements are attached to a ul node that is returned from the function. In view we simply call the renderList function and pass in the appropriate map from the model. See Listing 5-17.

Listing 5-17.

```
div [id "orderlist"] [
  renderList model.orders
]
```

The output of renderList is a node and is added to the div. This composition of functions is very powerful and lets us implement view in a way that can be maintained and tested easier than having everything in one big function.

You may have noticed that the function view returns Html msg. What does this mean? First, msg is in fact a placeholder for any type. We saw this in Chapter 3, but it is worth mentioning here because it is the source of some confusion.

Note   We see placeholders like msg in many places. They express an intent but are not necessarily meant to name an existing type. For example, model means that a defined model is supposed to be used, although we can name our models in any way as long as they start with an uppercase character. Sometimes, it would be better to use only a for placeholders to avoid confusion.

The parameter msg also means that we can pass *something* to our nodes. Of course, a message is meant, as we defined before. Assume a button that should run some code when updated. Let's create a button that sends the message AddOrder when clicked (Listing 5-18).

Listing 5-18.

```
div [class "pull-right", style [("padding-top","15px")]] [
    button [id "addtoorder", onClick AddOrder, class ("btn btn-default"
            ++ (defineAddOrderButtonState model.temporder.selected))]
            [text "Add to Order"]
]
```

The button defines in its attribute list the event callback onClick with the message AddOrder. The runtime will call our update function whenever that button is clicked. Then, the code in the appropriate case expression will update the model, and the runtime will again call view to render the page.

This way, we can use user input to change the state of the application, and thus the state of markup elements. The code in the AddOrder branch of update could, for example, set a model key with a value that disables the button. We don't need to do the call explicitly, just invoke a value change in our model.

The expression defineAddOrderButtonState model.temporder.selected is doing exactly that. It is a call to a helper function (Listing 5-19).

Listing 5-19.

```
defineAddOrderButtonState : PizzaOrder -> String
defineAddOrderButtonState selected =
  case String.isEmpty selected.pizza  of
    True -> " disabled"
    False -> ""
```

When a given predicate is met, the button will have the style class disabled attached and will not be clickable.

This dynamic behavior, together with the wiring in the background by the Elm runtime, is the power of the Elm platform.

subscriptions

Subscriptions are part of event handling in Elm. They are not necessary for small applications, although almost every more-complex application will have to use them.

The following example (Listing 5-20) defines that we are interested in `Keyboard` events and want to subscribe to them.

Listing 5-20.

```
type alias Model  =
  { k : Int
  }

type Msg
  = Key Keyboard.KeyCode

subscriptions : Model -> Sub Msg
subscriptions model =
  Keyboard.downs Key

update : Msg -> Model -> ( Model, Cmd Msg )
update msg model =
  case msg of
    Key code ->
      ({model | k = code } , Cmd.none)
```

The package `Keyboard` needs to be installed and imported to make this example work. We define a key k in the model and a message `Key`. The type `KeyCode` is an alias for an integer and is passed to our code when we subscribe to the `downs` event.

Our `subscription` function defines that we want to subscribe to the `downs` event, and then our `update` function with the message `Key` is called. In `update` we simply update our model with the key code. In a view, we could then display the value of the key code on the screen. Or, in the `update` function that handles the `Key` message, we could pass another command to the runtime that would then be run immediately; for example, to move an icon or sprite on the screen.

Subscriptions and *commands* look similar, and in fact they have one fact in common: they both are data. As commands are produced by the `update` function, subscriptions are produced by the Elm runtime. The `subscription` function is similar to the `update` function in that it handles messages.

We can subscribe to several events at once and will use this later in this chapter when we talk about user input.

Conclusion

In the previous sections we described the implementation of necessary callbacks for the Elm runtime when using the Elm architecture. It seems difficult to understand at first, but once we realize that many tasks are just running in the background without our intervention and we simply *declare* what we want the runtime to do, it will be clearer how it all works together.

Code Organization

So far in our simple examples we have had only one directory where all our files were saved. How can we organize an Elm application if there are many files and configurations involved? How can we organize our code to adhere to the Elm architecture?

The simplest way is to have all parts of the application in one file (Figure 5-3).

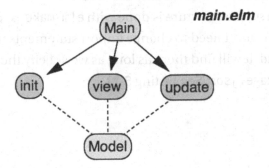

Figure 5-3. *Simple structure*

Here we have one file—main.elm—and access all functions and the model from within this file. Many examples you see will adhere to this structure.

Everything a little bit more complex will have separated files for the parts of the Elm architecture; otherwise, maintaining the code requires a lot of searching and scrolling. Figure 5-4 shows a file structure with more than one file.

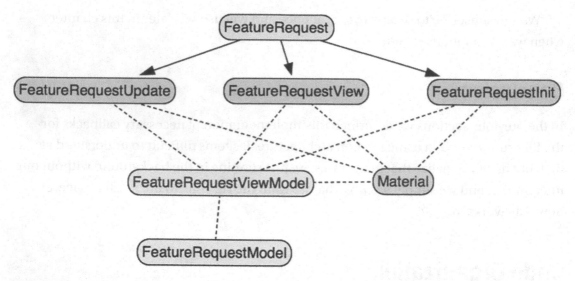

Figure 5-4. *Complex structure*

All the files in this figure are Elm code files except `Material`, which indicates a package that implements Material Design Lite for Elm.

This example is certainly extreme in separating all concerns. In fact, there are also folders called `init`, `model`, `update`, and `view` with corresponding files in them. All these folders are in a folder `src` where there is also `main.elm`.

A compilation with such a structure is done with `elm-make  src/main.elm`. In `main.elm` and in other files we don't need to change import statements to tell the compiler where files can be found. It will find them as long as we specify the correct source directories in `elm-package.json`. See Listing 5-21.

Listing 5-21.

```
...
"source-directories": [
        "src/model",
        "src/update",
        "src/view",
        "src/init"
    ]
...
```

If you use scaffolding templates, they may have their own view of the "proper" directory structure. There is no official directory structure. Some developers also experiment with separating by features, with `init`, `update`, and `view` files in each feature folder.

In any case, whatever structure you choose, stick to it across your projects to make your and your team colleagues' lives easier.

Rendering

As we described before, Elm is a platform for creating web applications. The packages that support building HTML are therefore very interesting for any developer using the Elm platform.

This section introduces the `Html` packages. We have already seen some of the methods in other examples. We remember that `Html` functions are used in the `view` function of our application, but also in all helper functions we build to make the `view` function easier to read.

Listing 5-22 shows a minimal view with a root div and one div with a header, a span, and a link.

Listing 5-22.

```
div [class "container"] [
    div [ class "jumbotron", style [("background-color","lightblue")] ] [
      h1 [] [ text "Pizza Ordering System" ]
      , span [style [("font-size","1.4em")]] [text "Example"]
      , a [href "#", style [("font-size","1.4em")]] [text "link text"]
      ]
]
```

Every *tag* in the listing is a function that is defined in the package `Html`. The attributes we see, like `style` and `href`, are defined in `Html.Attributes`.

The `Html` package has many helper functions that implement the most common HTML tags. All those functions take a list of attributes and a list of child nodes and return a node. Thus, tags can be nested, as we see in the example.

The tags `div`, `h1`, `span`, and `a` are all helper functions and are all in the list of the root div. The function `text` is a so-called primitive that takes a string and no attributes. Its output is plain text, which is escaped if necessary.

Plain text is great, but we want to do more—for example, render a list. If we have in our model a list—in our example, a list of `PizzaOrder`—we can create the helper function shown in Listing 5-23.

Listing 5-23.

```
renderList : List PizzaOrder -> Html msg
renderList l =
  ul[class "pizzalist"]
    (List.map (\item -> li []
        [span [class "pizzalistitem"] [text item.pizza ]) l)
```

This function returns `Html  msg` as functions in the `Html` package, so we can use it in the `view` function without changes. This is possible because we use one of the `Html` functions, `ul`. The parameter `l` is a list, and we just map over it, and in the closure we create an `li` tag for each element in the list.

To use the function, we just call it in the `view` function with the relevant type from our model as parameter. See Listing 5-24.

Listing 5-24.

```
div [class "container"] [
    h3 [] [ text "Pizza List" ]
    , renderlist model.pizzalist
]
```

So far, we have used common attributes like `class`, `style`, and `href`. There are many attribute functions defined in the package `Html.Attributes`, and it makes sense to look through the documentation to see if a certain attribute is already defined.

What happens if we want to use a custom attribute? For example, many JavaScript third-party libraries are using attributes like `data` or `v-for`. We can use the `attribute` function as in Listing 5-25.

Listing 5-25.

```
renderList : List PizzaOrder -> Html msg
renderList l =
  div[] [
      ul[attribute "v-if" ""]
```

```
      li [attribute "v-for" "item in items"] [text "{{ item.name }}"]
    , p [attribute "v-else" ""] [text "No items found"]
  ]
```

This is similar to the preceding example Listing 5-23 and uses the framework vue.js for rendering on the client. It is a rather contrived example, but shows the use of custom attributes.

Elm uses a *Virtual DOM* implementation to provide the functionality we saw in the view function. Similar to *React*[1], the Elm runtime manipulates an in-memory DOM and sends the changes to the browser. The package virtual-dom is mostly a *native* implementation, which means that parts are written in JavaScript.

There is no reason to use the virtual-dom package directly. The packages Html and Svg are higher-level APIs and make the declarative approach we have seen in the examples easily possible.

Graphics

We can tell Elm to render not only text, but also images and graphics. The simplest is to display an image. We can use a helper function the same way we use them for other HTML tags. See Listing 5-26.

Listing 5-26.

```
div [class "logotext mb-0"] [
    img [src "/static/images/pizza-icon.png", class "logo"] []
    , text "Pizza Cut"
]
```

As with all helper functions in the package Html, the function img takes attributes and a child node list. In the example, we see one of the attributes that is only valid in certain functions, src.

It is also possible to use CSS to display images (Listing 5-27).

---

[1]https://reactjs.org/docs/getting-started.html

Listing 5-27.

```
.container {
    margin: 1em auto;
    max-width: 800px;
    height: 600px;
    background-image: url('assets/bg.jpg');
}
```

Then, we can use this class in our Elm code in the function view. See Listing 5-28.

Listing 5-28.

```
div [ class "container" ] []
```

The browser will display the image as the background of the div we defined in Elm. Of course, this method can be used with HTML tags without Elm in exactly the same way.

More interesting is to use the canvas element of HTML5 and draw graphics directly in the browser. This is a more low-level method and is supported in the Elm platform very well.

The following example (Listing 5-29) simply draws a rectangle and fills it with a color. All the functions in the listing can be found in the package evancz/elm-graphics.

Listing 5-29.

```
div [] [
    toHtml <|
        container 400 400 middle <|
          collage 400 400 [
            rect 300 300
               |> filled (rgb 60 100 60)
          ]
]
```

The code makes heavy use of pipe operators to make the flow of computation more visible. The toHtml function transforms the internal presentation of the graphics into HTML that can be displayed in a browser.

The container function creates a wrapper element for the canvas, which is defined with the collage function. The collage defines width and height and takes a list of shape elements, like rectangles, polygons, and more. There are many functions in the package to manipulate those shapes. It also contains functions to render text and style it.

The declarative approach of the graphics package is powerful and can be used to create shapes interactively. Sometimes more scalable graphics or visualizations are needed, and this is where the package elm/svg comes in.

We saw an example of SVG in the first chapter. Elm's logo is defined as SVG, and the code is open sourced. Similar to HTML, all SVG functions take as parameters a list of attributes and a list of child nodes. The root node is built with the function svg. See Listing 5-30.

Listing 5-30.

```
main =
  svg
    [ version "0.9", x "0", y "0", viewBox "0 0 323.141 322.95"
    ]
    [ rect
        [ fill "#7FD13B", x "192.99", y "107.392", width "107.676",
        height "108.167"
        , transform "matrix(0.7071 0.7071 -0.7071 0.7071 186.4727
        -127.2386)"
        ]
        []
    ]
```

Creating SVG graphics requires studying the element reference to be able to create meaningful graphics. The Elm package implements these elements, and it will be necessary to create libraries on top of it for specialized graphics like visualizations.

Styling

Any non-trivial web application will have two features that go beyond simple HTML:

- JavaScript methods
- CSS styling

We will handle the first point later in this chapter; for now, we want to talk about styling. Generally, we have a three options to style our Elm application:

- Inline styles
- External CSS file
- Using a CSS framework

There is another option: using helper functions similar to the `Html` package. This approach has the advantage of having types that can be checked by the compiler. The disadvantage in an enterprise development environment is that designers won't touch Elm code. This leaves typed CSS helper functions for projects where the developer styles the application or where the time and effort to transfer CSS into Elm code is not seen as a negative.

Inline Styles

The helper function `style` is used in the `view` function to define inline styles. It is an attribute and takes a list of string tuples as arguments. See Listing 5-31.

Listing 5-31.

```
div [style [("padding-left", "30px")]] [
    h2 [style [("margin-top", "0px")]] [ text "All Orders"]
    , div [id "orders"] [
      ul [] [
        renderlist model.orders
      ]
    ]
]
```

The tuple list has elements with two strings, the first one being the key for the style, the second being the value. It is obvious that more style values will make the code eventually unreadable.

We could create helper functions for the styles to make the code in the function `view` easier to read. See Listing 5-32.

Listing 5-32.

```
wrapperdivStyle : Attribute msg
wrapperdivStyle =
    style
        [("padding-left", "30px")]

header2Style : Attribute msg
header2Style =
    style
        [("margin-top", "0px")]
```

Then, we can write the example as in Listing 5-33.

Listing 5-33.

```
div [wrapperdivStyle] [
    h2 [header2Style] [ text "All Orders"]
    , div [id "orders"] [
      ul [] [
        renderlist model.orders
      ]
    ]
]
```

Whether the inline styles are written directly or are used with a helper function does not change the fact—as we said about typed CSS libraries—that designers won't be able to change styles easily.

Inline styles are a bad practice and should not be used at all. It is sometimes handy to just put a style attribute into the code to test something out, but they should be externalized as soon as the test is done. It may be a good idea to have an optional compiler warning printed out if it encounters a style attribute.

External CSS

In web development, external CSS files are best practice and should be used for all Elm projects.

Testing or debugging our Elm application with elm reactor will see the external CSS only if we provide our own HTML file. We discussed how to do this in Chapter 2 and called this file Standalone HTML page. If we use this file again, we just need to add a link to our CSS file in the header. See Listing 5-34.

Listing 5-34.

```
<!DOCTYPE html>
<html>
  <head>
    <link rel="stylesheet" href="static/css/pizzaorder.css" />
  </head>
  <body>
    <script>
      if (typeof module === 'object') {
        window.module = module; module = undefined;
      }
    </script>
    <script src="./helloworld.js"></script>
    <script>if (window.module) module = window.module;</script>
    <script type="text/javascript">Elm.Hello.fullscreen()</script>
  </body>
</html>
```

With the standalone HTML file in place, we can then define the styles from the external file in our code with class attributes. See Listing 5-35.

Listing 5-35.

```
div [class "wrapperdivStyle"] [
    h2 [class "header2Style"] [ text "All Orders"]
    , div [id "orders"] [
      ul [] [
        renderlist model.orders
      ]
    ]
]
```

External CSS files don't provide type checking but are better suited for teamwork with developers and designers. Also, testing and style prototyping can be done with browser-based developer tools, which will improve turnaround.

CSS Framework

Most web projects don't build up styling from scratch; they use a framework. One of the most popular frameworks is *Bootstrap*.[2] Linking to Bootstrap is like using an external CSS file. See Listing 5-36.

Listing 5-36.

```
<!DOCTYPE html>
<html>
  <head>
    <link rel="stylesheet" href="static/css/bootstrap.min.css">
    <link rel="stylesheet" href="static/css/pizzaorder.css" />
  </head>
  <body>
    <script>
      if (typeof module === 'object') {
        window.module = module; module = undefined;
      }
    </script>
    <script src="./helloworld.js"></script>
    <script>if (window.module) module = window.module;</script>
    <script type="text/javascript">Elm.Hello.fullscreen()</script>
  </body>
</html>
```

We again use the standalone HTML page and add the link for the Bootstrap CSS file. We leave the project CSS file in for special styles or overwrites of Bootstrap styles. We can access all styles again with class attributes. See Listing 5-37.

---

[2]https://getbootstrap.com/

147

Listing 5-37.

```
div [class "container"] [
    div [ class "jumbotron jumbobg"] ] [
      h1 [] [ text "Pizza Ordering System" ]
    ]
]
```

Bootstrap styles in the example are container and jumbotron; jumbobg comes from the project styles file.

Using CSS frameworks makes development easier in most projects and—as with external CSS files—separates styling from the code in the Elm application that handles events and state.

User Input

In a previous section we discussed subscriptions to events. When a user presses a key or uses the mouse, an event will be created, and our code can handle this external event if subscribed to it.

Such events are not the only way to interact with an Elm application. The user can click on buttons, table rows, and similar. Those interactions will create internal events that are handled by the update function. See Listing 5-38.

Listing 5-38.

```
button [id "addtoorder", onClick AddOrder, class ("btn btn-default")]
    [text "Add to Order"]
```

The button in the example says that in case of a click event (onClick) the command AddOrder should be invoked.

Events are defined in the package Html.Events. Another example is onSubmit for forms, which we will see in code in the next chapter. There is also a function on that can be used to define custom events if there is a need for it.

We have seen in the section update in this chapter that commands are handled by the function update. When an onClick event occurs—the user presses the button—the Elm runtime knows that the message AddOrder should be sent to the application.

Two other user-input events were already mentioned, key input and mouse input. They are handled differently than the onClick event with the subscription mechanism. See Listing 5-39.

Listing 5-39.

```
type Msg
  = Position Int Int
  | Key Keyboard.KeyCode
  | Resize Size

subscriptions : Model -> Sub Msg
subscriptions model =
  Sub.batch
    [ Mouse.moves (\{x, y} -> Position x y)
    , Keyboard.downs Key
    , Window.resizes Resize
    ]
```

The example shows one new feature regarding subscriptions. We can subscribe to several events at once by sending a list of subscriptions to Sub.Batch. The events we subscribe to in the example are defined in the packages elm-lang/keyboard, elm-lang/mouse, and elm-lang/window. Defined in the packages are several functions we can use to subscribe to events. These functions also determine which arguments will be passed to our messages in case of an event.

We define in our type Msg the messages that will be passed to our update function. See Listing 5-40.

Listing 5-40.

```
update : Msg -> Model -> ( Model, Cmd Msg )
update msg model =
  case msg of
    Position x y ->
      ({model | x = x, y = y} , Cmd.none)
```

```
Key code ->
  ({model | k = code } , Cmd.none)

Resize size ->
  ({ model | size = size }, Cmd.none)
```

When the update function receives the messages from the subscribed events it simply updates the model. The application this code was taken from then displays the information in a status bar. See Listing 5-41.

Listing 5-41.

```
div [] [
    p [ class "background-header" ] [ Html.text ("Model: " ++ toString
    model) ]
    ]
```

Model: { x = 1391, y = 83, pegs = 5, backgroundimage = "bg.jpg", k = 18, size = { width = 1440, height = 781 } }

Subscriptions for user-interaction events are powerful and easy to implement. They are an elegant way to process side effects in a functional language.

JavaScript Interfacing

Any non-trivial Elm application will sooner or later need to interact with application-external JavaScript code. It is certainly possible to implement everything in Elm if enough time is available, but it is easier to use existing and tested code.

We used Bootstrap for styling, and it makes sense to also use the JavaScript components of this framework.

As before, we have to change our standalone HTML page (Listing 5-42).

Listing 5-42.

```
<!DOCTYPE html>
<html>
  <head>
    <script src="static/js/jquery-3.3.1.slim.min.js"></script>
    <script src="static/js/bootstrap.min.js"></script>
```

```
    <link rel="stylesheet" href="static/css/bootstrap.min.css">
    <link rel="stylesheet" href="static/css/pizzaorder.css" />
  </head>
  <body>
    <script>
      if (typeof module === 'object') {
        window.module = module; module = undefined;
      }
    </script>
    <script src="./helloworld.js"></script>
    <script>if (window.module) module = window.module;</script>
    <script type="text/javascript">Elm.Hello.fullscreen()</script>
  </body>
</html>
```

Interfacing with JavaScript means that a *pipeline* is needed between the Elm code and the JavaScript code in the browser. The mechanism is similar to the one we described for events. See Figure 5-5.

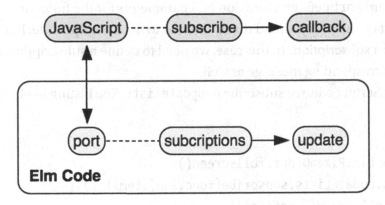

Figure 5-5. *Interfacing*

We can send data to JavaScript with ports and subscribe to it in the JavaScript code, or we can subscribe to data that is sent from JavaScript code to Elm code. In both cases, we get the data encoded, decoded, and type checked by the Elm runtime.

Ports are defined with the keyword port. Depending on if they are sending or retrieving data, the signature is slightly different. See Listing 5-43.

Note Ports must be defined in a module that is marked with `port` module `PizzaOrderUpdate exposing (..)`. It is recommended that only one module in an application be a `port` module.

Listing 5-43.

```
port setSize : (String -> msg) -> Sub msg
port updateLists : List String -> Cmd msg

type Msg
  = InputSize String

subscriptions : Model -> Sub Msg
subscriptions model =
  Sub.batch ([
    setSize InputSize
  ])
```

The keyword `port` defines a function and parameters for the function. If it sends data to JavaScript it creates a command that is listened to in JavaScript code. If it listens for data it creates a subscription. In this case, we need to define a subscription in the Elm code with a corresponding message as well.

In the JavaScript code, we subscribe to `updatelists`. See Listing 5-44.

Listing 5-44.

```
var elmapp = Elm.PizzaOrder.fullscreen();
elmapp.ports.updateLists.subscribe(function(itemlist) {
    $(document).ready(function(){
        // do something with the data
    });
});
```

The Elm compiler creates functions for `port` functions defined in Elm code, which we can use in our JavaScript code on the client. The function `subscribe` takes a callback as an argument that runs whenever we send data.

Note   The $(document).ready in the preceding example makes sure that updates are only done when everything is loaded. This is dependent on the framework used.

From Elm code, we send data to JavaScript by issuing a command (Listing 5-45).

Listing 5-45.

```
-- in update
-- helper function calculateOrder omitted

AddOrder ->
    let
        itemlist = calculateOrder model.temporder.selected
    in
        (m, updateLists itemlist)
```

The Elm runtime knows that updateLists is a port and forwards the data to the callback in the JavaScript code. If the JavaScript code wants to send data it uses the function send. See Listing 5-46.

Listing 5-46.

```
...
change: function (args) {
    elmapp.ports.setSize.send(args.value.toString());
}
```

The example shows a callback function from a textbox in the event of changed text. It gets the value from the textbox and sends it as a string to the Elm code. Since we subscribed to this event, a command will be created that is handled in the update function. See Listing 5-47.

Listing 5-47.

```
InputSize size ->
  let
      t = model.temporder
      m = Model {t | ordersize = size} model.orders  model.currenttime
  in
      (m, Cmd.none)
```

JavaScript interfacing in Elm uses patterns that are used in Elm code–only functions as well, which makes it easier to understand and implement.

Every data exchange with external sources like JavaScript code or HTTP requests can affect the state of the application if not restricted and handled carefully. It is still possible to crash an Elm application with external data, but the Elm runtime does its best to minimize the probability of failure.

Server Communication

Elm applications don't live on an island, but need to exchange data with sources that live outside Elm.

This section will discuss ways to exchange data with external servers. These may be REST servers or functions in a serverless environment over HTTP or exchange over other protocols like WebSocket.

To achieve communication with servers we need two things:

- We have to handle asynchronous requests and responses without blocking our application.

- We need a way to call services over HTTP.

The Elm platform provides functions for both HTTP requests and WebSockets. It also has a type Task defined in `elm-lang/core` that can be used to chain together HTTP requests.

HTTP

The package `elm-lang/http` has functions to create and send requests. Whatever HTTP verb we use, we always have to send a request to a URL and process the response in our update function.

The signature for the `http.send` function needs some explanation. See Listing 5-48.

Listing 5-48.

```
send : (Result Error a -> msg) -> Request a -> Cmd msg
```

The function takes two parameters. The first is a function that wraps the result of the `send` operation in a message. This result can be a failure or a success. The second describes an HTTP request and can be of any type. In Elm code, we would write the expression shown in Listing 5-49.

Listing 5-49.

```
Http.send ImageName (Http.getString "http://localhost:8080")
```

The first parameter is one of our messages we define in the union type with the name `Msg` or similar. The second parameter is a function call to a given URL. When the result of the `getString` request is received, the message `ImageName` will be sent to the update for processing.

The preceding explanation left out some important details we will discuss in the following sections.

GET

The simplest request is to get string data from a server and process it. We have just seen this code in a more generic form, but the following example (Listing 5-50) is how it would be done in an application.

Listing 5-50.

```
getImageName : Int -> Cmd Message
getImageName id =
  let
    url = urlImage ++ (toString id)
  in
    Http.send ImageName <| Http.getString url
```

This function first creates a dynamic URL with an image ID as argument and then uses this URL to get the name of the image. Instead of passing the request as an argument, we pipe the result into the `send` function.

The message ImageName is then sent to the update function (Listing 5-51).

Listing 5-51.

```
ImageName (Ok imagename) ->
    ({model | imagename = imagename}, Cmd.none)

ImageName (Err d) ->
    case d of
        Http.BadPayload s _ ->
            ({model | status = "Error getting image name: " ++ s}, Cmd.none)
        _ ->
            ({model | status = "Error getting image name"}, Cmd.none)
```

We remember that the function send wraps the result in a message and can indicate that the request either failed or was successful. This is why we need to implement both cases.

The Ok case is straightforward, and in this case we just update the model. The Err case checks if there is more information as to why the request failed. Http.BadPayload is one of a few defined error types. In the first argument, we get a status code with which we update the model. This example ignores the second argument, which is the body of the response. We also ignore other error types and only set a generic failure status in the model.

Normally, we will try to retrieve more complicated data than a string. To do this we will use the more general function get. See Listing 5-52.

Listing 5-52.

```
getImagesList : Cmd Message
getImagesList =
  let
    url = urlImage
  in
    Http.send Image <| Http.get url decodeImage
```

This code is similar to the earlier code when we retrieved the image name string, but there is one big difference. The get function needs a decoder function, in our case decodeImageList. We need to tell Elm which data we expect and how to get from the response body data to the Elm type. See Listing 5-53.

Listing 5-53.

```
Image (Result Http.Error ImageEntity)

type alias ImageEntity =
  { id: Int
  , url: String
  , name: String
  }

  decodeImage : Decoder ImageEntity
  decodeImage =
    map 3 ImageEntity
      (field "id" int)
      (field "url" string)
      (field "name" string)
```

We briefly looked at JSON decoders and encoders earlier in this book. This decode function looks difficult to grasp at first, but it makes sense once we explain it.

We want to get the metadata for one image. This data is retrieved from a server, and we will get JSON data in the response body. We know which Elm type (ImageEntity) this JSON data should represent. So, we take the raw data from the response and process it with the function decodeImage. This function only knows how to transform data from JSON to an Elm type.

The function map3 in the preceding example combines several decoders—in our example they are all string decoders—and creates a type of Decoder ImageEntity. The number at the end of map indicates how many decoders can be combined. The map* functions run from map1 to map8, so JSON data with more fields must be handled in a different way.

The decoder function is like a template for http.get. At the end, the message Image is sent with an argument of type ImageEntity if the decoding has been successful.

The preceding example produces only one entity; if we want to create a list we can do so with the expression in Listing 5-54.

Listing 5-54.

```
decodeImageList : Decoder (List ImageListEntry)
decodeImageList =
  map 3 ImageListEntry
    (field "id" int)
    (field "name" string)
    (field "creator" string)
  |> Decode.list
```

The difference from the single entity is that we create a list of entities with the function `Decode.list`. This function can also be used to transform a list element in one entity; for example, `(field "contributorlist" (list string))`.

POST

Posting data to a server from the Elm application is done similar to receiving data (Listing 5-55).

Listing 5-55.

```
    Http.send ImageMetaData <|
        Http.post "http://localhost:8080/images" Http.emptyBody (list
string)
```

The preceding example posts an empty body to the local server and provides a decoder for the response body. Most of the time this simplified solution with the function `post` is not used in favor of the more generic `request` function (Listing 5-56).

Listing 5-56.

```
    Http.request
        { method = "POST"
        , headers = []
        , url = "http://localhost:8080/images"
        , body = jsonBody (encoderImage ImageEntity)
        , expect = expectJson decodeImage
        , timeout = Nothing
        , withCredentials = False
```

```
        }

encoderImage : ImageEntity -> Encode.Value
encoderImage image =
    Encode.object
        [ ( "id", Encode.int image.id )
        , ( "url", Encode.string image.url )
        , ( "name", Encode.string image.name )
        ]
```

This version has many more options and will be used for other requests in the next section as well. The example creates a request body with JSON data. To send the correct data we have to encode the Elm type.

Encoding is a similar pattern to decoding. The encoded value is built up by combining encoders for different types. The resulting value can then be passed to jsonbody.

We assume in this example that the server returns the sent image in the response body, perhaps with the field id updated to the value corresponding to the database entry. This is why we have to tell the request to expect JSON data and why we also provide the decoder we used before to decode the response body.

The function request can also be used for other HTTP verbs like PUT or PATCH or for advanced features like multi-part bodies or authorization request headers.

WebSockets

Apart from HTTP requests, connections to a server can also be done via the WebSocket protocol. Of course, this requires a server that understands the protocol.

WebSockets can be used for interactive or multi-user applications where data is pushed to the clients dynamically and asynchronously.

Clients subscribe to incoming data ("events") from the server—a pattern that reminds us of previous event subscriptions from having discussed user interactions or JavaScript interfacing. And, indeed, in Elm WebSockets are implemented as subscriptions. See Listing 5-57.

Listing 5-57.

```
subscriptions : Model -> Sub Msg
subscriptions model =
  WebSocket.listen "ws://localhost/8081" ReceiveMessage
```

We subscribe to a local WebSocket server (for example, `Node.js WebSocket library`[3]), and our update function will receive a `ReceiveMessage` message. See Listing 5-58.

Listing 5-58.

```
ReceiveMessage str ->
  ({model | ServerMessages = str :: ServerMessages}, Cmd.none)

SendMessage msg ->
  (Model, WebSocket.send "ws://localhost/8081" msg)
```

In `ReceiveMessage` we add the message from the server to our message list in the model.

We also define a message for sending to the WebSocket server with `SendMessage`. This may be sent after user input and a click on a button. The Elm implementation of `WebSocket` also takes care of queuing messages to the server if the connection is lost.

What We Learned

This chapter discussed the Elm architecture in detail and how to organize our code. We also looked at several building blocks for our applications, as follows:

- Rendering
- Styling
- User input
- JavaScript interfacing
- Server communication

It is time now to apply our knowledge and dissect a complete example application.

---

[3]`https://github.com/websockets/ws`

CHAPTER 6

Putting It All Together

In this chapter, we will apply the knowledge gained in this book so far to create a single-page application. We will also look at possible usages of Elm beyond web applications.

Building a Single-Page Application

A *single-page application* (SPA) is a web application that loads a single HTML page. It can be more or less static, or it can have dynamic updates triggered by user interactions.

Most of the work in an SPA happens on the client side. This can be a browser on a desktop or mobile device, or a wrapper like Electron or another cross-platform framework. Data processed in the application is transferred to and from backend servers via protocols like HTTP.

Our example application is an SPA that shows how to use features of the Elm platform, discussed in previous chapters, and bind them together in one application. We will use, among others, the following:

- Rendering HTML elements

- Processing user-interaction events

- Styling with a JavaScript library

- HTTP requests

- Handling JSON

Pizza Cut—The Application

So, what is our example application? It is *Pizza Cut*. Let's assume we are tasked with developing a form for an online pizza order web app. This form is for the internal use of pizza employees who take orders over the phone. We assume that all orders—once

© Wolfgang Loder 2018
W. Loder, *Web Applications with Elm*, https://doi.org/10.1007/978-1-4842-2610-0_6

confirmed—will be sent to the kitchen and that the cooks will go ahead and bake the ordered pizza.

The flow is as shown in Figure 6-1.

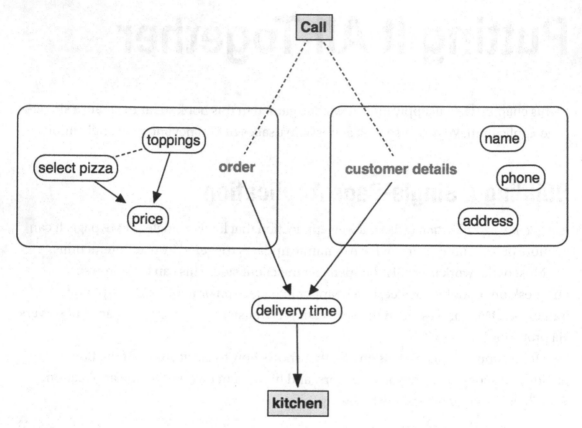

Figure 6-1. *Application overview*

When a call comes in we will get two pieces of information—the actual order and the details of the customer.

Getting the order just involves selecting a pizza and its toppings. The price will be automatically calculated and displayed. Customer details are name, address, and phone number.

Once all information has been gathered, a delivery time can be estimated and displayed.

Specifications are as follows:

- Select a pizza from a drop-down list. Unavailable pizzas should be grayed out.

- Once a pizza is chosen, additional toppings can be added, depending on the selection in the drop-down list.

- The price updates dynamically, depending on pizza and toppings selected.

- It is possible to choose more than one pizza for each order.

- There are name, address, and phone fields, with validation for the phone field.

- No order can be submitted if not all fields in the customer form are filled out.

- Depending on address and pizza selection, an approximate delivery time will be displayed.

- We assume payment on delivery.

- Submitting the form updates an order list that is displayed in an additional tab.

- The backend server calculates price and delivery time and processes the order list.

Our backend server is a web API server implemented with Elixir and Phoenix. On the client we use Bootstrap 4 to make the UI prettier, and we will also use Bootstrap's JavaScript components.

Design

Keeping the requirements in mind, the design of our application looks like the images in the following figures. First, the *Take Order* form looks like Figure 6-2.

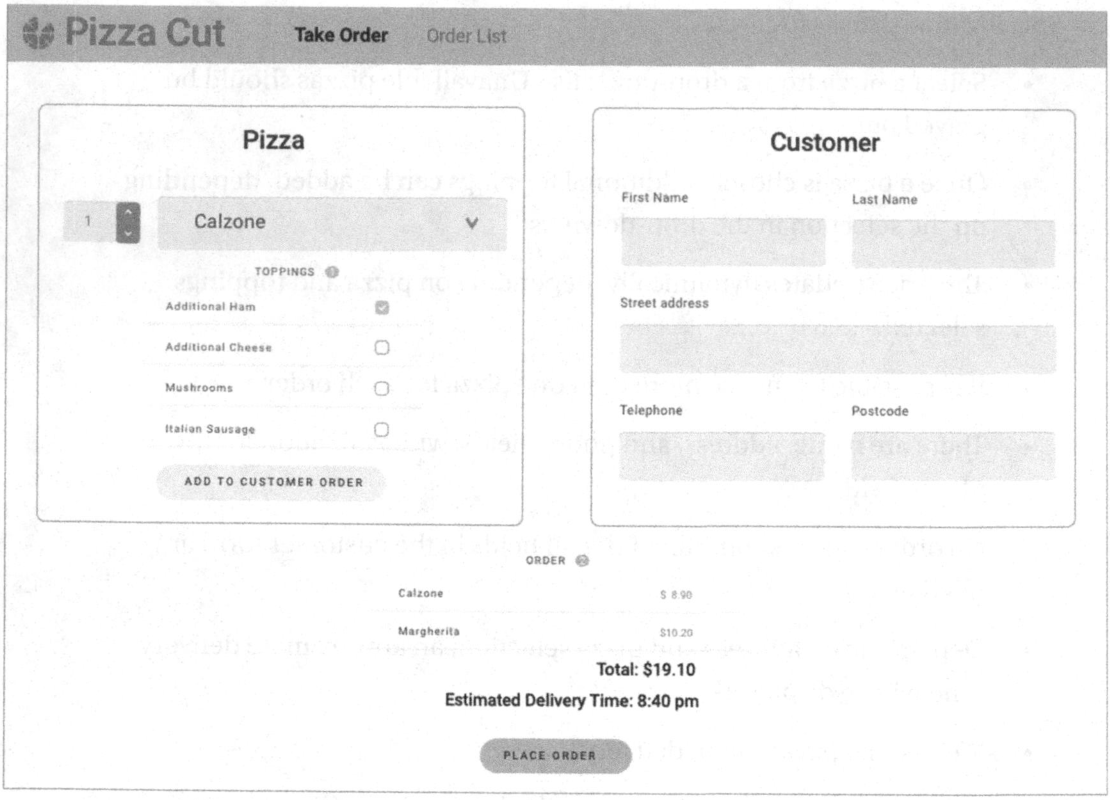

Figure 6-2. *Form—Take Orders*

At the top left we have all the information regarding the order; at the top right is the form for a customer's information. The part below the top forms is updated dynamically, with the button only showing as enabled when all information is in the form and validated.

When orders are placed, the second screen shows the order list with delivery times. This list is supposed to be viewed by managers and the cook. See Figure 6-3.

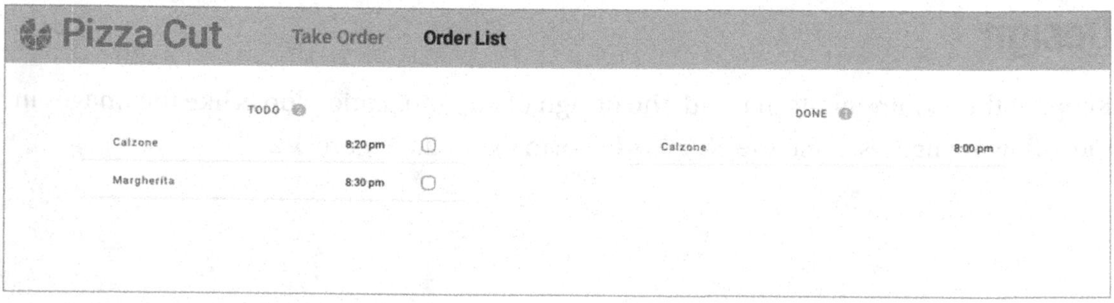

Figure 6-3. *Form—Order List*

It shows two lists, one for upcoming orders and one for already fulfilled orders. These lists have only one interactive element, which is the checkbox to indicate that a pizza is ready. Then, the entry on the left will be moved to the *Done* list with an updated time.

Alternative Specification and Design

As with all specifications and designs, there are decisions that could be made in a different way. Many such decisions were driven by showing certain Elm platform features as they could be used "in the wild."

We use the backend for tasks that could be done on the client side, like estimating delivery times or calculating prices. The idea behind this is that there may be more than one client feeding data into the backend. This, of course, would affect estimations and calculations.

Some developers may oppose having tabs be used in our application, which in some circles is not seen as pure SPA. The simple answer is that we use it to show how navigation in Elm works.

Using Bootstrap's JavaScript components may result in opposition from some developers who like to stay in the Elm platform. There is a good reason for it; for example, type checking and staying within one paradigm. In real life, project managers wouldn't be persuaded by that argument, as they would just want a fast way to go into production. And, by using third-party JavaScript components we can show JavaScript interfacing from Elm very well.

Implementation

Now, our task is to implement the application as it is designed with all the features listed in the specifications. The implementation will be *similar* to the design sketches. In a business environment the designer would certainly make us reimplement the application until it is exactly like the design, but for this app we assume that *similar* is sufficient.

This is a book about Elm, so we won't go into an explanation of how the backend is implemented. The backend exposes an API with the following routes:

- /api/orders (POST)
- /api/orders?filter=pending (GET)

- /api/orders?filter=fulfilled (GET)

- /api/estimatetime (GET)

- /api/calculateprice (GET)

Note   Our backend is not a REST API and does not want to be. It mixes nouns and verbs, but it does the job for this example application. The additional query parameters also give us the chance to discuss custom HTTP requests in Elm.

The POST route takes a JSON argument in the body, and all routes return JSON. Although we do not discuss the backend code, it is available in the code download of this book.

Our implementation will make use of the Bootstrap 4 libraries. All could be done in Elm without external CSS or JavaScript files, but this would not be a real-world situation. Most probably the project you work for has its own standards, design languages, and the like. The Elm application—which may be only part of a site or even a page—will have to consider these restrictions.

Setup

First, we want to set up our project. We will start with an elm-package.json file and define dependencies (Listing 6-1).

Listing 6-1.

```
"dependencies": {
        "elm-lang/core": "5.1.1 <= v < 6.0.0",
        "elm-lang/html": "2.0.0 <= v < 3.0.0",
        "elm-lang/http": "1.0.0 <= v < 2.0.0",
        "elm-lang/navigation": "2.0.0 <= v < 3.0.0",
        "elm-lang/keyboard": "1.0.1 <= v < 2.0.0",
        "elm-community/elm-time": "1.0.1 <= v < 2.0.0",
        "elm-community/list-extra": "6.0.0 <= v < 7.0.0",
        "krisajenkins/formatting": "4.2.0 <= v < 5.0.0"
    },
    "elm-version": "0.18.0 <= v < 0.19.0"
```

Apart from the standard libraries, we use community packages to make dealing with time and lists easier. For time formatting, we use a package that provides type-safe string formatting.

Our folder structure is geared toward separation of code into logical folders. See Figure 6-4.

Figure 6-4. *Application folder structure*

All code files are in src. The folder static contains CSS files, JavaScript files, and image assets. Tests for the application are in the folder tests.

The application has very descriptive names for Elm code files to show that this is possible as well. It is not necessary, but keeps it very clear which modules are imported.

Along with the usual view, update, and model files, there is also a file called
`PizzaOrderBusinessLogic` with implementations of a few helper functions that deal
with business logic on the client side.

As we are linking to external frameworks, we need to create a standalone HTML page
to start our application. See Listing 6-2.

Listing 6-2.

```
<!DOCTYPE html>
<html>
 <head>
 <title>Pizzeria - Elm Example</title>
  <script src="static/js/jquery-3.3.1.slim.min.js"></script>
  <script src="static/js/popper.min.js"></script>
  <script src="static/js/bootstrap.min.js"></script>

  <link rel="stylesheet" href="static/css/bootstrap.min.css">
  <link rel="stylesheet" href="static/css/pizzeria.css" />

  <link rel="icon" type="image/png" sizes="32x32" href="static/images/
   favicon-32x32.png">
  <link rel="icon" type="image/png" sizes="96x96" href="static/images/
   favicon-96x96.png">
  <link rel="icon" type="image/png" sizes="16x16" href="static/images/
   favicon-16x16.png">

  <script src="PizzaOrder.js" type="text/javascript"></script>
 </head>
 <body>
  <div id="embeddedelm"></div>
  <script type="text/javascript">

    let elmapp = Elm.PizzaOrder.fullscreen({
      dummyflag: 0
    });

  </script>
 </body>
</html>
```

We include CSS for Bootstrap 4 and also the necessary JavaScript files for Bootstrap components. In addition, we keep an application-specific file for styling that goes beyond Bootstrap or overwrites its styles.

Note   The image file links are favicon files for different resolutions and sizes.

When we develop we don't want to compile or run the application manually. This is why we create a package.json file to integrate commands in the scripts section and run it with npm run. We mentioned this method in Chapter 2. See Listing 6-3.

Listing 6-3.

```
"scripts": {
    "cd": "elm make src/PizzaOrder.elm
            --output PizzaOrder.js --debug --yes",

    "cdw": "elm make src/PizzaOrder.elm
            --output PizzaOrder.js --debug --warn --yes",

    "c": "elm make src/PizzaOrder.elm --output PizzaOrder.js --yes",

    "rp": "elm repl",

    "r": "elm reactor --port 3505",

    "watch": "chokidar '**/*.elm' -c 'elm make src/PizzaOrder.elm
        --output PizzaOrder.js --warn' --initial",

    "watchd": "chokidar '**/*.elm' -c 'elm make src/PizzaOrder.elm
        --output PizzaOrder.js --debug --warn' --initial",

    "tdd": "chokidar '**/*.elm'
        -c 'node_modules/elm-test/bin/elm-test' --initial",

    "inittests": "cd tests; elm package install --yes",

    "t": "node_modules/elm-test/bin/elm-test"
},
```

```
"devDependencies" : {
  "chokidar-cli": "^1.2.0",
  "elm-test": "^0.18.2"
}
```

The main idea is to use chokidar to watch the src folder of the application and then compile the code. We can compile with or without the debug flag.

In another terminal window, we can run npm run r and open a browser window at localhost:3505. Alternatively, we can use, for example, live-server[1] at the root level of the application, which updates automatically when an output file like pizzaorder.js or a CSS file changes.

Included in the scripts is a tdd command that can be run in an additional terminal window to run tests whenever an Elm code file changes. There are also compile and run commands to perform these tasks without watching folders and files.

Package.json is also needed to install the community test runner for Elm, elm-test. There will be more about this in the section "Testing."

Now that we have explained the setup of our application, we can discuss the main parts of the implementation and how they work together.

Model

Our model has two sides, the client side in Elm and the backend side in the backend in Elixir. The latter communicates directly to the database, in this case a PostgeSQL database.

The backend database implementation is a relational schema while the client Elm model is kept relatively flat. We decided to have a set of DTOs (data transfer objects) in Elm to iron out mismatches between client and backend.

The client model looks like Listing 6-4.

Listing 6-4.

```
type alias PizzaOrder =
  { number: String
  , pizza: String
  , toppings: List String
  , size: String
  }
```

---

[1]https://www.npmjs.com/package/live-server

```
type alias Customer =
    { name: String
    , address: String
    , telephone: String
    , ordered: List PizzaOrder
    , selected: PizzaOrder
    , time: String
    , amount: Float
    }

type alias Model  =
  { temporder: Customer
  , orders: List PizzaOrder
  , currenttime: String
  , flags: Flags
  , page : Page
  , history : List Navigation.Location
  }
```

The model is nested and has some fields like temporder to keep the state of the application.

We also define all the messages that will be used in the application. Some of them we will see in subscriptions to communicate between JavaScript components and the Elm code, while others are in response to user-interaction events and still others are application internal. See Listing 6-5.

Listing 6-5.

```
type Msg
  = NoOp
  | AddOrder
  | ConfirmOrder
  | CancelOrder
  | InputName String
  | InputAddress Strin
  | InputTelephone String
  | InputOrderNumber String
```

171

```
| InputPizza String
| InputTopping String
| RemoveTopping String
| IncrementQuantity
| Quantity String
| CurrentTime Time
| UrlChanged Navigation.Location
| NewUrl String
```

The NoOp message is not necessary but helps during development as a placeholder for unimplemented commands.

Navigation

The application uses tabs, so we need a way to switch between those tabs. In Elm we can use the package elm-lang/navigation to handle "pages" in a single-page application.

All the code to implement navigation can be found in different code files (Listing 6-6).

Listing 6-6.

```
-- in model
type Page =
  Home
  | Orders

type alias Model  =
  {
    -- leaving out some fields...
  , page : Page
  , history : List Navigation.Location
  }

-- in update
    UrlChanged location ->
      { model | page = (getPage location.hash) } ! [ Cmd.none ]

    NewUrl url ->
      (model, Navigation.newUrl url)
```

```
-- helper function
    getPage : String -> Page
    getPage hash =
        case hash of
            "#home" ->
                Home
            "#orders" ->
                Orders
            _ ->
                Home
```

The Page type is defined for convenience to have a current-page indicator in our state, and the history field in the model is used for the Back button. In our case, it is not really necessary, but it is good to have the data in case the application gets changed to a multi-page application later.

When we use the navigation package, we get a message whenever the URL changes. The update function in our application handles this in such a way that we change the state of the application by setting the page field to the page that was requested.

We call the helper function getPage with the hash of the requested URL as argument. The hash is exactly what we would get from document.location.hash in JavaScript. In getPage we can define which page is requested and return the correct value from our union type Page. If there is no recognized hash passed in we always return Home.

How does the Elm runtime know that we should get the message UrlChanged? The application entry function main needs to be changed. It still calls the same Html. program or Html.programWithFlags, but we have an additional layer. The navigation package provides the same functions, and when we call it, it adds the message to the subscriptions we specify.

Our application uses flags as well, which does not affect the main function regarding navigation. See Listing 6-7.

Listing 6-7.

```
main : Program (Maybe Flags) Model Msg
main =
  Navigation.programWithFlags UrlChanged
    { init = init
    , view = view
    , update = update
    , subscriptions = subscriptions
    }

init : Maybe Flags -> Navigation.Location -> ( Model, Cmd Msg )
init flags location =
  let
    initialstate =
      case flags of
        Maybe.Just flags ->
          {initialModel | flags = (Flags flags.availableorders), history =
          [location] }
        Nothing ->
          initialModel
  in
    (initialstate , Task.perform CurrentTime Time.now)
```

The second change has to be applied to the `init` function. Apart from the argument
`flags`, it also has a `location` argument. This is necessary so as to have a default page and
a valid location history.

One last thing remains: How do we request a new URL? We do this in the function
`view` when we click on a tab header.

The following code (Listing 6-8) shows a part of the code in the helper function
`renderNavbar` for the default tab (`home`).

Listing 6-8.

```
renderNavbar : Model -> Html Msg
renderNavbar model =
  case model.page of
    Home ->
```

```
div [] [
    div [class "container-fluid topbar"] [
        nav [id "topbar", class "navbar navbar-expand-lg navbar-light
        bg-faded"] [
            div [class "logotext mb-0"]
                [img [src "/static/images/pizza-icon.png",
                class "logo"] []
                , text "         Pizza Cut"]
        , div [id "navbarNav", class "collapse navbar-collapse"] [
                ul [class "navbar-nav"] [
                    li [class "nav-item"] [
                        div [class "activetab"] [text "Take Order"]
                    ]
                    , li [class "nav-item"] [
                        a [class "nav-link inactivetab", href "#orders",
                            onClick (NewUrl "/orders") ] [text "Orders"]
                    ]
                ]
            ]
        ]
    ]
]
```

The link with the hash #orders has an onClick event defined and sends a message NewUrl with the requested URL. The relevant expression in the update function then calls Navigation.newUrl, which in turn updates the location history and sends the message UrlChanged.

Navigation in Elm is a good example of the event-driven nature of programming with the Elm platform. It is a little bit difficult to understand at first when coming from an imperative-programming background. After a while, the event-driven and declarative paradigm becomes clear, and we let the Elm runtime do its job.

Main View

The view in our application is not very complex, but it is still difficult to follow the code when it is all written in one function. Our main function is therefore very short. See Listing 6-9.

Listing 6-9.

```
view : Model -> Html Msg
view model =
  div [] [
    renderNavbar model
    , renderPage model
  ]
```

We just tell the Elm runtime to call to render functions. The first one, renderNavbar, we saw earlier, at least one part of it. The second one, renderPage, has two parts wrapped in a case expression.

The first case is for the home page, the default tab. See Listing 6-10.

Listing 6-10.

```
renderPage : Model -> Html Msg
renderPage model =
  case model.page of
    Home ->
      div [class "container-fluid pagebody"] [
        div [class "row"] [
          div [class "col-4 border border-dark rounded mt-3 ml-4 mr-5"][
            div [class "mx-auto titlefixed"] [text "Pizza"]
            , Html.form [] [
              div [class "form-group"] [
                renderPizzaSpinner model
                , renderToppingSelect model.temporder.selected
                , div [class "input-group"] [
```

```
                    button [class "btn btn-success btn-sm",
                            type_ "button",
                            onClick AddOrder] [text "ADD TO CUSTOMER ORDER"]
                ]
            ]
        ]
    ]
    , div [class "col-4 border border-dark rounded mt-3 mr-4"] [
        div [class "mx-auto titlefixed"] [text "Customer"]
        , Html.form [] [
          div [class "form-group"] [
            label [for "firstname"] [text "First Name"]
            , input [id "firstname", class "form-control"] []
          ]
        ]
      ]
    ]
  ]
-- ...
```

Many Bootstrap CSS classes are used to style the markup. It is organized in two columns, with a form in each column. Again, two helper functions make the code more readable.

The function renderPizzaSpinner will be used later in the section form, so we won't show it here. The function renderToppingSelect is a form with checkboxes. It calls itself the helper function renderToppingList to list all toppings for a pizza selection. See Listing 6-11.

Listing 6-11.

```
renderToppingSelect : PizzaOrder -> Html Msg
renderToppingSelect p =

  div [class "", id "toppingsselect"] [
    div [class "mx-auto titlefixed-toppings"] [text "TOPPINGS"]
    , renderToppingList p.toppings
  ]
```

This implementation of renderToppingList is similar to what we saw in Chapter 5. We use List.map to create the markup for the list. We also call another function for the item markup and code. See Listing 6-12.

Listing 6-12.

```
renderToppingList : List Topping -> Html msg
renderToppingList l =
        (List.map (\item -> renderToppingListItem item) l)

renderToppingListItem : Topping -> Html msg
renderToppingListItem t =
    div [class "form-check"] [
        input [class "form-check-input", type_ "checkbox", value "",
        id t.id] []
        , label [class "form-check-label", for t.id] [text t.name]
    ]
```

The second tab displays a list of orders. It is not different from the list mapping we have done before, so we won't show the code of the function renderOrderList. You can see it in the downloaded application code. See Listing 6-13.

Listing 6-13.

```
Orders ->
    div [class "container-fluid pagebody"] [
        text ("Orders for today @ " ++ model.currenttime)
        , div [class "row"] [
            renderOrderList model.orders
        ]
    ]
```

The view code for our application is separated into several functions. For small applications this is a little more work, but all applications grow in features, and this separation will make it easier to maintain and enhance the code for the views.

Forms

Most applications need a form in some way. Login and register forms are obvious candidates, but we also have search or preferences forms. In any case, we have to define a model for the form, some validation mechanism if needed, and callbacks in our code for when the form is submitted.

Forms in Elm are straightforward to implement as long as you are not interfacing with the outside world. In this section, we will follow one form element through the Elm code.

Earlier, we saw the spinner element, which was used to adjust the number of a pizza that will be ordered. The function `renderPizzaSpinner` provides the markup for this element.

We have implemented the decrement and increment buttons in different ways to show both a pure Elm approach and a JavaScript approach. See Listing 6-14.

Listing 6-14.

```
renderPizzaSpinner : PizzaOrder -> Html Msg
renderPizzaSpinner p =
  div [class "input-group", id "pizzaspinner"] [
      span [class "input-group-btn btn-group-sm"] [
        button [class "btn btn-success", type_ "button",
          attribute "data-action" "decrementQtyPizza"]
          [text "-"]
      ]
    , input [name "quantity", type_ "text",
        class "form-control text-center",
        value p.quantity, attribute "min" "1"] []
    , span [class "input-group-btn btn-group-sm"] [
        button [class "btn btn-success", type_ "button",
          onClick IncrementQuantity] [text "+"]
    ]
  ]
```

The increment button works by sending the message `IncrementQuantity` to the update function. See Listing 6-15.

179

Listing 6-15.

```
update : Msg -> Model -> ( Model, Cmd Msg )
update msg model =
  case msg of
    IncrementQuantity ->
      let
        t = model.temporder
        s = t.selected
        qu = toString ((Result.withDefault 0 (String.toInt s.quantity))+1)
        s_ = {s | quantity  = qu}
        m = Model {t | selected = s_}
          model.orders
          model.currenttime
          model.flags
          model.page
          model.history
      in
        (m, Cmd.none)
```

The handling code of the message IncrementQuantity needs to first do some housekeeping and then just updates the quantity in the model for the selected pizza. Since data in Elm is immutable, we need to create a new PizzaOrder for the field selected and update the model with it.

What's interesting is the expression qu = toString ((Result.withDefault 0 (String.toInt s.quantity))+1). Actually, we can be sure that the quantity can be converted to an integer, but we code here defensively. If the conversion fails it will return the default value 0.

Interfacing with JavaScript Components

As previously mentioned, the decrement task of the spinner element is done in JavaScript. Before we show the code for this, let's look at all the JavaScript interfacing this application uses.

There are several subscriptions defined that update the state of the application upon user interactions. Again, these state updates could be done completely within Elm if all elements were implemented in Elm. On the other hand, we want to use third-party

JavaScript components, and it would be ineffective in some projects to reinvent the offered features. See Listing 6-16.

Listing 6-16.

```
port updateLists : String -> Cmd msg

port setNumber : (String -> msg) -> Sub msg
port setPizza : (String -> msg) -> Sub msg
port setTopping : (String -> msg) -> Sub msg
port removeTopping : (String -> msg) -> Sub msg
port setQuantity : (String -> msg) -> Sub msg

subscriptions : Model -> Sub Msg
subscriptions model =
  Sub.batch ([
    setNumber InputOrderNumber
    , setPizza InputPizza
    , setTopping InputTopping
    , removeTopping RemoveTopping
    ,
  ])
```

We won't get into all the JavaScript code in the file index.html. In fact, the handling is always similar. The component on the client side either listens to an event from the Elm code or invokes an event in the Elm code.

The port updateLists goes to the client code. JavaScript code listens to this event like in Listing 6-17.

Listing 6-17.

```
elmapp.ports.updateLists.subscribe(function(itemlist) {
    // ...
}
```

In Elm code, we set off this event in the update function when an order is added (Listing 6-18).

Listing 6-18.

```
AddOrder ->
    let
        -- ...
        itemlist = calculateOrder model.temporder.selected
    in
        (m, updateLists itemlist)
```

The reason we do it like this is that we want to feed the data into a grid component on the client side.

Coming back to the spinner component, we have the following JavaScript code to decrement the quantity (Listing 6-19).

Listing 6-19.

```
$(document).ready(function(){
  $('#pizzaspinner').find('button').on('click', function(){
    let input = $(this).closest('#pizzaspinner').
    find('input[name=quantity]');

    if($(this).data('action') === 'decrementQtyPizza') {
      if(input.attr('min') === undefined
        || parseInt(input.val()) > parseInt(input.attr('min'))) {

        input.val(parseInt(input.val(), 10) - 1);
        elmapp.ports.setQuantity.send(input.val().toString());
      }
    }
  });
});
```

The code relies on two attributes. We defined the button in Elm with one attribute. See Listing 6-20.

Listing 6-20.

```
button [class "btn btn-success",
        type_ "button",
        attribute "data-action" "decrementQtyPizza"]
    [text "-"]
```

The attribute data-action has the value of decrementQtyPizza to indicate the action that should be taken when this button is pressed. The data- attributes are standard when defining custom data that can be used in JavaScript. In our JavaScript code we only act on a button if this attribute is set and has a known value.

We also defined the input field with one important attribute. See Listing 6-21.

Listing 6-21.

```
input [name "quantity", type_ "text",
    class "form-control text-center",
    value model.temporder.selected.quantity,
    attribute "min" "1"] []
```

The attribute min indicates the minimum input value for this element. In our JavaScript code we use this value to ensure we do not decrement below this value.

Once we have established that the value needs to be decremented, we do so, and we also call the Elm code with elmapp.ports.setQuantity.send(input.val(). toString()) to give it the opportunity to update its state. Otherwise, the value would only be changed on the client side, and a refresh would show the old value.

The subscription says setQuantity Quantity, so when the event setQuantity arrives the message Quantity is sent. The model is updated, and then the view function will display the correct value. See Listing 6-22.

Listing 6-22.

```
Quantity number ->
        let
            t = model.temporder
            s = t.selected
            s_ = {s | quantity = number}
```

```
    m = Model {t | selected = s_}
       model.orders
       model.currenttime
       model.flags
       model.page
       model.history
  in
    (m, Cmd.none)
```

JavaScript interfacing in Elm is straightforward to implement. It should be used sparingly, if possible, but if there is a need to do it, then there is a way. Attention should be directed to values coming from JavaScript code. Even with type checks in Elm there is no guarantee that the value is correct, especially if string types are often used.

Also, JavaScript interfacing needs to have well-tested code on the client side that an application can rely on; otherwise, even Elm applications can fail at runtime.

Testing

Tests are part of application development, and the Elm platform provides a framework for it. We have seen in this book that debugging an Elm application is not always easy. More unit tests and regression tests need to be incorporated in the development.

The community has provided a test package and also a test runner. All tests are in their own folders and have their own configurations with special dependencies. See Listing 6-23.

Listing 6-23.

```
"dependencies": {
        "elm-community/json-extra": "2.0.0 <= v < 3.0.0",
        "elm-lang/html": "2.0.0 <= v < 3.0.0",
        "mgold/elm-random-pcg": "4.0.2 <= v < 5.0.0",
        "elm-lang/core": "5.0.0 <= v < 6.0.0",
        "elm-community/elm-test": "3.0.0 <= v < 4.0.0",
        "rtfeldman/node-test-runner": "3.0.0 <= v < 4.0.0",
        "elm-lang/http": "1.0.0 <= v < 2.0.0",
        "elm-lang/navigation": "2.0.0 <= v < 3.0.0",
```

```
      "elm-lang/keyboard": "1.0.1 <= v < 2.0.0",
      "elm-community/elm-time": "1.0.1 <= v < 2.0.0"
   },
    "elm-version": "0.18.0 <= v < 0.19.0"
```

The dependencies for our application are not only the test packages, but also language and library packages that are needed to run the tests. These dependencies also need to stay in sync with the application dependencies to ensure the compatibility of tests with the application.

In the root folder of our application we have to install elm-test with npm install elm-test. We could add the -g flag to install it globally. Then, we run run elm-test init, and a folder tests is created with a default elm-package.json, a file tests.elm, and a file main.elm, which is the entry point for running the tests. See Listing 6-24.

Listing 6-24.

```
port module Main exposing (..)

import Tests
import Test.Runner.Node exposing (run, TestProgram)
import Json.Encode exposing (Value)

main : TestProgram
main =
    run emit Tests.all

port emit : ( String, Value ) -> Cmd msg
```

The file main.elm won't be changed, but the file tests.elm will contain the tests for our application. We see that the function main calls Tests.all. This is the function in tests.elm in the module Tests. See Listing 6-25.

Listing 6-25.

```
module Tests exposing (..)

import Test exposing (..)
import Expect
import Fuzz exposing (list, int, tuple, string)
import String
```

```
import PizzaOrderBusinessLogic exposing (..)
import PizzaOrderModel exposing (..)

all : Test
all =
    describe "Pizza Order Test Suite"
        [
            describe "BusinessLogic"
                [ test "calculateOrderNumber Default" <|
                    \() ->
                        Expect.equal 2 (calculateOrderNumber initialModel)
                , test "calculateOrder Model" <|
                    \() ->
                        Expect.equal "text: 0" (calculateOrderNumber
                        initialModel)
                ]
        ]
```

Like in other test frameworks, elm-test knows to expect functions, and the tests can be organized in suites and have descriptions for printing out information during test runs. The body of a test is implemented with closures.

One special feature in elm-test is the inclusion of *fuzzy tests*, in other frameworks also called *property tests*. Input into functions is randomized, and the tests are run a minimum of times. This exposes the function to various conditions, and if there is no failure emerging then the confidence into a positive test is greater.

Beyond Elm Web Applications

The Elm platform has a central purpose: writing web applications—mostly single-page applications—with a functional language. So far in this book we have seen that it can do this well within the constraints of a platform that is evolving and may still change, even in core functionality, over the next few years.

Learning a new language is time consuming, so the question is legitimate as to whether Elm can be used to implement projects other than web applications. In the last few years there has been a trend to bring JavaScript and languages that transpile to

JavaScript to the backend and develop both frontend and backend processes with one language. Elm is transpiled to JavaScript, so maybe it can be used in the same way.

In the following sections we will examine the possibility of using Elm on desktop, command-line, and integrating it with other web frameworks.

Desktop Applications

A few years ago it seemed that desktop applications were a thing of the past. One of the main reasons for this was that developing for different platforms was and still is too expensive, either for initial development or maintenance. There were early efforts to create multi-platform frameworks, the most known among them being Java and Flash. Neither approach yielded the expected results, so they were not used much outside of corporations, games or development tools.

A change came with the success of Node.js and faster JavaScript engines. Not only was it possible to write web applications in JavaScript, but it was also possible to wrap the whole web application, including a browser, to be executable for different platforms. When GitHub used this method to create their open source code editor *Atom*,[2] more developers took advantage of this idea. Eventually, the core of the editor was open sourced as Electron, which forms the basis for several applications, like Slack and others.

Two of the biggest arguments against Electron apps are the memory footprint and speed. The memory footprint is especially problematic when more than one Electron app is running; for example, on a developer machine that may be on the edge with IDEs, containers, and others in the memory of a machine that may have only 16 GB or even less.

Note   Electron apps have frameworks included in every app, especially a full Chromium, which is a runtime environment and is almost an operating system, not just a web browser. Those apps need at least 130 MB but can go up to 1 GB and more. It is important to know that every webview used in an Electron application uses a new copy of the aforementioned runtime.

Electron exposes some system services of each platform, like file access, and the JavaScript code in an Electron application communicates with the Electron runtime. Since Elm is compiled to JavaScript, we can use it to write a desktop application.

---

[2]https://github.com/atom/atom

The source code for this book has an example in the directory Examples/Elm-Electron. Open a command line in that directory and run the commands in Listing 6-26.

Listing 6-26.

```
npm install
npm run start
```

This will start the Electron application with a simple Elm program. Let's now examine how we can implement this.

I assume that Electron is installed on your machine. Their website[3] has download links for all platforms to install Electron globally, or you can use the pre-built package in the npm repository for a local install, as the example does.

First, we have to create a folder for the application and in that create a package.json file. Listing 6-27 omits some key–value pairs that are not essential for the example.

Listing 6-27.

```
{
  "scripts": {
    "start": "electron ./app",
    "postinstall": "install-app-deps",
    "pack": "build --dir",
    "dist": "build"
  },
  "devDependencies": {
    "electron": "1.7.10"
  },
  "build": {
    "productName": "Elm-Electron-Example",
    "appId": "elm-electron-example"
  }
}
```

---

[3]http://electron.atom.io/

We defined the `electron` package as a development dependency and added `scripts` and `build` sections. The latter is necessary for Electron to build the application. Scripts are not really necessary but help with development. I should point out that this way to set up an Electron application is the bare-bones way. More sophisticated ways involve setting up a project with a *Yeoman* generator and also using *Gulp* for development tasks. Have a look at the Awesome-Electron[4] list.

Our way of organizing the code is to have the root directory as the *development directory* and to have an `app` directory for the actual source code. This implies that we have a second `package.json` in the `app` directory to define values—especially dependencies—for the application code. See Listing 6-28.

Listing 6-28.

```
{
  "main": "./index.js"
}
```

Again, I omitted the non-necessary key–value pairs. It turns out that we have only one relevant key since there are no dependencies defined. The `main` key has `./index.js` as the value that tells Electron which code to run when starting. Actually, Electron defaults to `index.js` as the entry point of the application, so we would not need to spell this out in the configuration. It is possible to have any other file name, and then this entry would be needed.

When we ran the `npm start` command before, we ran a script with the line shown in Listing 6-29.

Listing 6-29.

```
electron ./app
```

The argument for the call is `.app`, which passes to the Electron program the directory in which to look for the main entry point.

A quick remark about the file `renderer.js` in the app directory. Electron uses more than one process. The `main*` process is the one that runs the main script—in our case, the code in `index.js`. This process then creates `renderer` processes for each web page that is used in the application. These GUI processes are sandboxed and cannot share

---

[4]`https://github.com/sindresorhus/awesome-electron`

data between them, except by communication with the main process or by using HTML5 features like local storage.

So, how do we get the Elm code into Electron? It is the same as running an Elm application in any other browser. Our main process tells the Electron runtime to create a browser window and render index.html. Listing 6-30 shows the code to create the browser in index.js.

Listing 6-30.

```
function createWindow () {
  mainWindow = new BrowserWindow({width: 1024, height: 780})
  mainWindow.loadURL(`file://${__dirname}/Index.html`)
  mainWindow.on('closed', function () {
    mainWindow = null
  })
}

app.on('ready', createWindow)
```

When the Electron runtime calls the ready callback it runs the function createWindow. This function creates a browser window and loads the file index.html. See Listing 6-31.

Listing 6-31.

```
<!DOCTYPE html>
<html>
 <head></head>
 <body>
   <script>if (typeof module === 'object')
      {window.module = module; module = undefined;}
    </script>
   <script src="./elm.js"></script>
   <script>if (window.module) module = window.module;</script>
   <script type="text/javascript">Elm.GamesFramework.fullscreen()</script>
 </body>
</html>
```

We know the contents of this file from previous examples. The code file `elm.js` is the one we create in whatever Elm project we want to use. We could have more than one page, with the code coming from different Elm applications, but Electron works best as a single-page application.

How do we use Electron's API calls, like getting the contents of a file? We use *ports* as we would in a web application in a non-wrapped browser. So, it is easily possible to wrap an existing Elm application and distribute it as an Electron app.

CLI

Wouldn't it be nice to use our knowledge of Elm to write small utilities that could be invoked from the command line? Elm compiles to JavaScript, but also needs its runtime and libraries. The resulting code file—as we saw in previous explanations—is a few hundred KB big depending on the used libraries, but this is not a problem on the desktop. Our task is to find a way to call Elm functions that were compiled into JavaScript from JavaScript outside Elm.

Node

My first idea was to use Node and create a Node CLI application, similar to Electron.

The first problem with this approach is that the Elm runtime needs to be started. In early versions this was possible without browser integration, but the runtime is now more restrictive. The idea behind this is that the Elm platform is a web application platform and is not thought of as a general-purpose platform. Also, calling from outside into Elm-based functions may cause some problems with types, as we know. The compilation can check the Elm code, but it is not possible to check outside arguments without a resource-expensive analyzing process at runtime.

The second problem is that the asynchronous Elm runtime collides with the asynchronous event handling of Node when no web server is used. With a web server this is not a problem, but it goes against the idea of a CLI program.

The idea is to call the following function (Listing 6-32) in Elm from a Node function.

Listing 6-32.

```
module ShellScript exposing (..)

someFunction : String
someFunction =
  "Hi from an Elm function"
```

This is just a placeholder function to test the concept. We want to call this function from a Node script and display the returned string in the console. We already know that it is not possible to call it directly, but we can use ports as in the Electron application. The only question is, how do we get a browser window that we don't want to display? We could use *jsdom*,[5] a DOM implementation for Node.

The idea was good, but it does not work. With jsdom I could embed a page with the JavaScript compiled by Elm, but the Node code could not communicate with the code in the embedded page. In any case, even if it had worked, the whole solution is too much of a hack to be viable.

The conclusion is that, at the moment, we cannot use Elm with Node to create a CLI application.

REPL

We don't need to give up on our task—to use an Elm application from the command line—because we have the REPL. Unfortunately we cannot run `elm-repl` with a parameter to say which module we want to import, but we can work around this.

The idea explained in this section came from a small Perl script that helps keep text and code examples in sync.

It takes a regular expression pattern and replaces every positive found, like `example-1-0`, with the file contents of a file that has the name of the positive (`example-1-0`).

If we wanted to transfer this one-line script—which is available in the download—to Elm and look for packages to use, we would immediately see a big problem. With the current version of Elm it is not possible to read or write files. Well, we will still implement the replacement, but we have to get the input markdown text from a module, and we will output to the console.

---

[5]`https://github.com/tmpvar/jsdom`

The module FixCode does the regular expression search and replacement (Listing 6-33).

Listing 6-33.

```
module FixCode exposing (..)

import Chapters exposing (..)
import ShellScriptLib exposing (..)
import CodeExamples exposing (..)

defaultPattern : String
defaultPattern = "example-[0-9]-[0-9][0-9].(txt|elm|json|js|html)"

replaceExampleCode : String -> String
replaceExampleCode markdown =
  let
    md = readMarkdownFile markdown
    poslist = getPositivesListDefaultPattern md
  in
    replace poslist md

replace : List String -> String -> String
replace poslist markdown =
  case poslist of
  [] ->
      (markdown)

  first :: rest ->
    let
      newmd = replaceText first (getsubstitution first) markdown
    in
      replace rest newmd

readMarkdownFile: String -> String
readMarkdownFile name =
    getChapter name
```

```
getPositivesListDefaultPattern : String -> List String
getPositivesListDefaultPattern text =
  getPositivesList
    defaultPattern
    text

getsubstitution : String -> String
getsubstitution positive =
  getCodeExample positive
```

Since we can't read from a file, we have to read from a module, which is done with the functions getChapter and getCodeExample. We are not printing these two functions, because all they do is return text that will be substituted.

The function replace in the preceding listing is a recursive function processing the list of all positives and printing out the resulting string in the console. Unfortunately, no file can be written at this moment.

The module ShellScriptLib contains the functions that deal with the regular expressions. The pattern example-[0-9]-[0-9][0-9].(txt|elm|json|js|html) is passed in as argument to replaceText, which calls the Regex.replace function in the package elm-lang/core. See Listing 6-34.

Listing 6-34.

```
module ShellScriptLib exposing (..)

import Regex exposing (..)
import List exposing (..)

replaceText : String -> String -> String -> String
replaceText pattern substitution text =
  text |>
    Regex.replace All (regex (pattern)) (\_ -> substitution)

getPositivesList : String -> String -> List String
getPositivesList pattern text =
  map.match <| find All (regex pattern) text
```

In getPositivesList we apply the closure that finds a pattern in a text and create a list of strings to be processed as positives later.

This finishes our discussion of Elm beyond web applications. There will be more to discover when the Elm platform matures and workarounds for some problems we encountered in this section can be found.

What We Learned

This chapter discussed some aspects of a full Elm application. We saw the specifications and design of the application and got deeper into implementation aspects like the following:

- Setup

- Creating a model

- Navigation

- Views

- JavaScript interfacing

- Testing

We also took a look at whether we could use Elm for more than web applications, like the following:

- Desktop applications

- Command-line utilities

This book gave an introduction into the Elm platform. In the last chapter, we will see where Elm might go in the future.

CHAPTER 7

Where to Go from Here

This book has given you an introduction into building web applications with the Elm platform. Now you know the basics of Elm and have seen some of the most important libraries at work in code examples. As mentioned in the first chapter, there is much more to learn to make the Elm platform productive for bigger projects.

We have only scratched the surface of the platform. The Elm language has more to offer than what we have discussed, such as the following:

- Multi-module applications
- Handling state changes between modules
- Encoding and decoding complicated JSON
- Optimizing function parameters for piping
- Type constructors
- Implementing features like authentication and validation in Elm
- Implementing functional patterns

In this list we have not even mentioned those functions in the standard library we did not discuss in this book, nor some of the many helpful community libraries.

Elm is an evolving language and platform, and so are standard and community libraries. One of the biggest features in Elm is static typing. More and more packages are created to provide type-safe integrations for JavaScript libraries or CSS patterns like Material Design.

197

© Wolfgang Loder 2018
W. Loder, *Web Applications with Elm*, https://doi.org/10.1007/978-1-4842-2610-0_7

When Is a Programming Language and Platform Successful?

Based on discussions with other developers over the years, it seems that there are a few criteria to make a programming language popular and thus successful, as follows:

- Advantage over existing stacks

- Enhancing developer productivity

- Easy to learn

- Easy-to-maintain code

- Glamour and appeal by offering a different approach to existing languages

- Reducing complexity

Certainly the Elm platform has a few of these points ticked off: enhancing productivity, appeal, and reducing complexity. Of course, the learning curve may be higher if you are coming from an imperative language paradigm or a mixed paradigm like the one JavaScript implements. Elm is functional, but once learned it makes development easier.

Not everything is rosy, though. Especially as an enterprise developer, you need to have good arguments to convince management to use the Elm platform. We need to keep in mind that Elm is in the alpha stage of development. It may have gained a good amount of attention, but the platform still has a way to go. This needs to be taken into consideration when recommending Elm to management.

Language Progression

The Elm language is changing on a regular basis, and the version number indicates that with versions numbered way below the golden 1.0 release. Along with the language, libraries and concepts are also changing. We explained in this book that the Elm architecture went through a development process. The same applies to the standard libraries.

When you look into online discussions about Elm you will see several feature requests that are regularly mentioned, as follows:

- Tree shaking and dead-code elimination

- Module functors

- Type classes

- Union types as keys in Dict

- Higher-kinded polymorphism

I am aware that this book is for beginners of the language—probably also for beginners in functional programming. So, terms like *functors* or *type classes* may not make much sense. They make clear, though, that there is a big interest from functional programmers, especially those developing with or having knowledge of Haskell. We mentioned it before: sometimes Elm is like an entry step into studying Haskell. It is not a Haskell Light, but it takes many ideas from it and is, of course, implemented in Haskell itself.

The most probable feature of the preceding list that will be implemented soon is *tree shaking*. We have mentioned that for every embedded Elm application we have to supply all the runtime and any library the Elm code is accessing. So, if we embed three Elm applications in a web page, we will have to download three times the runtime. At the moment, all of the runtime and all of the libraries are in the JavaScript file the Elm code compiles to.

Other languages and frameworks provide some sort of tree shaking, which means that untouched code will be deleted from the final *executable*. For example, we can do this in JavaScript with WebPack.[1]

A feature beyond tree shaking would be to have a runtime that the compiled Elm code can link to. This would make caching in the browser and avoiding unnecessary HTTP requests easier.

In all these discussions about features, we should not forget that Elm was initially a language for rendering graphics in a browser and then evolved into a framework to make single-page applications and the rendering of their markup more effective and error free by using static typing. Elm was not supposed to be a multi-purpose language or a complicated framework like others in the web development realm.

---

[1]https://webpack.js.org/guides/tree-shaking/

Community

Every programming language depends on the community of developers who use the language and often develop new concepts not imagined by the language creators. Languages and frameworks heavily backed by big companies did not always use the power of developer communities. For example, it took Microsoft a long time to open their .NET framework up and accept contributions from outside the company. Similarly, in the Java world languages on top of the JVM are thriving almost more than the original language; for example, Scala or Clojure. In the functional world, the emerging language Elixir had a similar effect on the Erlang VM.

Elm's community is very active and interested in bringing the platform forward. Sometimes this may be against the plans of the language creator, but eventually the different interests will come together for the good of the platform.

Commercial Usage

The big question is if the Elm platform is ready for commercial use. Some companies are using it for their applications or at least for a part of their applications. There is an unknown number of other companies that use Elm for internal or customer applications as well.

The preferred way to introduce Elm into a project is to do it slowly and just for parts of a website. This may be one way to integrate Elm into an application and having management agree, because the risk of failure is minimized.

Another criteria for commercial usage is to be able to maintain the code. Finding Elm developers is not easy, especially experienced ones. This may be an obstacle, as is the long time between Elm platform releases and the lack of possible fixes and patches for existing versions.

The Future

Like everyone else, I don't have a crystal ball to look into the future, so the following thoughts are best guesses. Examples in the JavaScript community have shown that fashions change quickly. Not long ago, Angular was the most loved framework, but then suddenly Reactive has taken over almost completely. Is it the backing of Facebook or the slow development and breaking changes and concepts of Angular 2? Is it the preferred use of Typescript in Angular 2? Or is it the reactive concept?

The Elm platform has great potential. Although it is good that the hype is restricted, Elm needs to have clear roadmaps and at least some deadlines for upcoming features. Otherwise, developers will use Elm for pet projects, but without clear planning they won't be able to commit for bigger projects.

Conclusion

We have arrived at the end of this book. I hope you take it as an appetizer and will keep the Elm platform in mind when you have to choose a language and framework for your next project.

Index

© Wolfgang Loder 2018
W. Loder, *Web Applications with Elm*, https://doi.org/10.1007/978-1-4842-2610-0

Printed in the United States
By Bookmasters